FOCUS on PhOnicS

FOCUS on PhOniCS

Assessment and Instruction

Wendy Cheyney and E. Judith Cohen

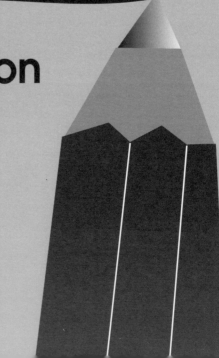

Wright Group McGraw-Hill

19201 120th Avenue NE • Bothell, WA 98011

Focus on Phonics: Assessment and Instruction

Text copyright ©1999 Wendy Cheyney and E. Judith Cohen
Copyright ©1999 The McGraw-Hill Companies, Inc.

Wright Group/McGraw-Hill
19201 120th Avenue NE
Bothell, WA 98011
www.WrightGroup.com

Printed in Hong Kong

10 9 8 7 6 5 4 3

ISBN 0-322-00762-3

Library of Congress Cataloging-in-Publication Data

Cheyney, Wendy S.
    Focus on phonics : assessment and instruction / Wendy Cheyney and E. Judith Cohen.
        p. cm.
    Includes blibliographical references.
    ISBN 0-322-00762-3 (paper spiral bound)
    1. Reading--Phonetic method. 2. Reading (Early childhood) 3. Reading (Elementary)
    I. Cohen, E. Judith, 1949- II. Title.

LB1050.34 .C44 2000
372.46'5--dc21   00-043321

To our loving husbands and children.
For Wendy, this book is dedicated to her husband Frazier
and their daughters Siri, Kim, Melissa, and Kristi.
For Judy, it is to her husband Ken
and their daughter Julie and son David.

Contents

Part 1

Chapter 1. The Conceptual Framework 1

Chapter 2. Focus on Phonics 7

Chapter 3. Phonological Awareness: Hear It 13

Chapter 4. Print Awareness: See It .21

Chapter 5. Graphophonic Analysis: Associate It 27

Chapter 6. Structural Analysis: Expand It 37

Preface

This book is but one small contribution to the literature on language and literacy instruction, but it is one that is intended to broaden teachers' perspectives as well as their practice. In Focus on Phonics, we discuss some of the current issues that teachers wrestle with daily, particularly as they facilitate the growth of language and literacy in children. We focus in this volume on the assessment and instruction of phonics, but we must emphasize to readers that phonics instruction is only one part of a comprehensive literacy program. In developing our perspectives, we placed a strong emphasis on keeping great literature in the forefront of great instruction. By building instructional strategies for decoding that relate to children's literature, we encourage skill development that will bring joy to the processes of listening, speaking, reading, and writing. When all aspects of a language and literacy program are inextricably woven together, each component must be strong enough to support and expand the others.

The evidence strongly supports the idea that fluent language and literacy learners use a number of cueing systems simultaneously. Phonics is one of the most influential of these cueing systems because of its basis in the auditory verbal language system. The auditory processing system provides an oral language foundation that includes phonology, semantics, and syntax. These same components provide the basis for other forms of literacy development (reading and writing).

Focus on Phonics approaches the teaching of phonics from a developmental perspective. We suggest that phonics should be taught not as an isolated skill, but as an integrated part of a comprehensive program of language and literacy instruction. Because of the connection to verbal language, we refer to the earliest instruction as *prephonics*. Unfortunately, many teachers of early childhood programs omit this prephonics instruction and begin phonics instruction with synthetic phonics (sound-symbol associations). We provide both assessments and instructional objectives that focus initially on the development of phonological and print awareness, which are foundational prerequisites for phonics instruction. Furthermore, we suggest that when this later synthetic phonics instruction is started, it should be taught simultaneously with analytic phonics. This enables the reader to "sound out" a word, say the word as a recognizable whole, comprehend its meaning, and see the pattern. Combining synthetic and analytic phonics enables the reader to internalize the pattern and therefore decode more automatically in subsequent readings. When early literacy experiences focus on listening and speaking as well as reading and writing, teachers have many wonderful opportunities to provide instruction in phonological and print awareness while they and their students enjoy poems, stories, songs, and rhymes.

Part 2 of this book provides assessments, student profiles, and coded lesson plans to demonstrate intervention strategies. These materials are not meant to be regarded as a complete program, but rather as a collection of model, or prototype, activities that are linked to poems, songs, rhymes, and stories frequently used in shared and guided reading. A teacher can easily expand on or adapt these lessons to be used with other materials. For those teachers who prefer a more formal, structured intervention we recommend The Wright Skills program (available from The Wright Group), which includes a comprehensive Prephonics components, as well as three levels of Phonics and Word Study. All four Wright Skills kits use literature as a basis, and all activities are meaningful and sequential.

In summary, language and literacy acquisition is a highly complex task, at best, and presents a true challenge for many children. It is crucial to remember that phonics, although it is only one of the four cueing systems that fluent readers use, is basic to literacy because of its direct link to language. In the search for balance in reading programs, we must guide students to "conquer the code" (the alphabetic code of the language) so that they will be able to "master the meaning" (comprehension). Our hope is that teachers will modify, adapt, and extend the ideas presented in this book as they strive to share the gift of reading with students everywhere.

Acknowledgments

This book is the result of a wide variety of teaching and learning opportunities in the course of many years. As we have developed our thoughts and perspectives over time, there have been many teachers, students, friends, and professional colleagues who have influenced, encouraged, supported, and taught us. Probably our greatest teachers have been the children we chose to devote our careers to—children with mild, moderate, and severe learning disabilities. These children have taught us about patience, flexibility, openness to new ideas, and an appreciation that almost anything can be accomplished with loving support and a willingness to pursue our goals.

We have both been blessed with a great deal of love to share with others, and we have found many career opportunities that afforded us the chance to blend our knowledge and our caring. Therefore, we are sincerely grateful to each and every child, parent, teacher, friend, and colleague who so unselfishly assisted us in becoming who we are today. In working with several thousand teachers in the last three years alone, we were able to see the results of the material included in this book, and with that came again the opportunity for us to grow, to change, and to refine our thoughts.

We extend a special thank-you to Dr. Donna Brewer of The Wright Group, for she alone heard us, made a decision to listen, and believed we could change children's lives by focusing on phonics, even if just for a while. Also, a special thanks to the many publishing professionals who helped us edit, polish, and publish this manuscript.

Introduction

When test scores are not commensurate with expectations, school districts often buy more instructional products in an effort to solve the problem. However, new materials may not necessarily result in better instruction. Teachers are the most important variable in the ultimate effectiveness of instructional strategies and materials. For this reason, this book begins with teachers, providing them with ways to implement and assess phonics skills instruction using stories and other print already available in their classrooms. Most classrooms have rich and varied stories and other materials for children to read. We encourage teachers to explore ways to use these materials more effectively for teaching phonics skills.

The chapters in Part 1 address the *code it*, or phonics, part of a balanced reading program. Part 2 consists of assessment items and lesson plans teachers can use to initiate phonics lessons. Each assessment level has an overall plan for a balanced reading lesson and lesson plans for teaching each component of phonological awareness, print awareness, synthetic phonics, analytic phonics, and structural analysis. A blank copy of each lesson format is included in Appendix 1.

Chapter 1

The Conceptual Framework

Different pedagogical philosophies offering a variety of models, methods, and approaches have influenced present-day reading instruction. A great deal of research has been conducted to determine the most effective approaches to teaching early reading to both typical learners and at-risk learners. The data—controversial, oppositional, and confusing at times—have led reading educators to vacillate among a range of popular methods. Educational journals often publish articles focusing on philosophical debates such as behaviorism versus constructivism, holistic versus traditional models, bottom-up versus top-down theories, and meaning-based versus code-based approaches. These debates have raged for many years. For example, in the late 1960s, Chall's *Learning to Read: The Great Debate* (1967, 1983, 1989) examined the controversy about whether children should be taught to read with a *sight* approach or a *phonics* approach. This controversy is echoed today in the hot debate over the merits of instruction described as *whole language* versus the merits of instruction that begins with phonics.

The Behaviorist Reading Instruction Model

In the common *behaviorist model* of the "reading readiness" era, skills instruction was initiated apart from whole texts, and skills were practiced in isolated workbook or worksheet activities. In this model, teachers placed little or no emphasis on practicing skills in context, resulting in poor skill retention.

When skills are learned apart from meaning, they are usually stored in short-term rather than long-term memory. This short-term storage makes it more unlikely that children will be able to retrieve and apply the newly acquired information. To store new knowledge in long-term memory, the learner must have a need to learn it. Then the learner must associate this new knowledge with prior knowledge, or *schema*, already stored in long-term memory. Next, the learner must have many opportunities to practice the skill in meaningful situations. And last, he or she must participate in activities and experiences that allow for transfer and generalization. In other words, to effectively acquire, store, and retrieve new knowledge such as reading skills, the learner must first have a purpose for learning it, be provided with many opportunities to practice it, and ultimately apply it in other related situations.

The Balanced Reading Instruction Model

Some recently proposed reading instruction models are based on cognitive psychology. These newer models suggest that young children experience emergent literacy beginning at birth and that literacy development continues throughout their school experience. These models also take into account ideas from cognitive psychology about long- and short-term memory and the way information is stored. We advocate an inclusive and balanced approach to early literacy education and believe that phonics instruction is central to such an approach. The *balanced reading instruction model* is based on cognitive psychology. While the behavioral reading instruction model basically focuses on parts and the synthesizing and blending of those parts into meaningful wholes, the balanced reading instruction model focuses more on the interaction of the learner with print.

Teachers following this model employ a whole-to-part-to-whole approach. As Strickland

(1998) explains, teachers engage children in reading by initially focusing on their comprehending and enjoying a given story, poem, song, chant, or rhyme. Using whole text instead of isolated parts of text emphasizes the content of literature and provides opportunities to teach skills within meaningful contexts. As teachers listen to children reread the text, they assess children's learning and teach appropriate skills and strategies in relation to the text. Additional skills may be taught "out of context" but are eventually reapplied to the original text. When children recognize that the purpose of skills instruction is to help them make sense of print, their learning becomes concrete and meaningful. Skills taught in meaningful contexts are more likely to be remembered and transferred to new print situations.

As shown in Figure 1.1, a balanced reading instruction model includes instruction in both the alphabetic code and meaning. This instruction, at times, may be explicit, direct, and systematic. While some children may learn to read in an implicit manner, teachers need to balance instruction according to students' needs. Therefore, skills instruction may include both in-context and out-of-context activities.

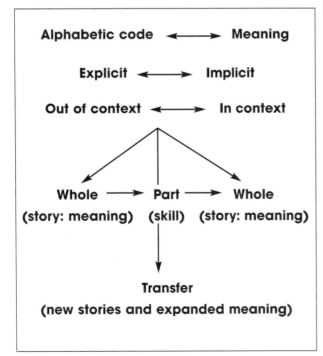

Figure 1.1 The Balanced Reading Instruction Model

The Recursive Reading Process

While the behavioral reading instruction model is linear, the balanced reading model is recursive, resembling the model used as a basis for the writing process movement. In the recursive writing process, the learner begins by developing an idea for a story. After this prewriting experience, the learner writes a first draft and then rereads and rewrites it until it is ready for editing. Once the editing is complete, the document is ready for publishing.

Reading may also be perceived as a process. Through inquiry, the teacher moves the learner through a prereading experience that expands already existing knowledge and creates and develops new ideas. Vocabulary is presented through discussion rather than as an isolated skill. As the teacher and learner read the story, the emphasis is on enjoyment and comprehension of the story as a whole. Rereading allows for reflecting, discussing, questioning, observing details, analyzing characters, and so on. Finally, the teacher provides opportunities for the learner to respond to the story through an activity that is closely related to the story's content. The teacher then presents the skill lesson in connection with the story, providing a meaningful context for learning and allowing for more generalization. After the children practice the skill, they have opportunities to apply it in a familiar text before transferring it to novel print.

In summary, this type of reading model begins with a prereading activity, proceeds to the enjoyment of the story as a whole, returns to the text to highlight a skill or part, provides skill or part practice, and ultimately prepares the learner to apply and transfer this knowledge to new stories and novel print situations. This recursive process allows for expansion of meaning as well as greater opportunities for application and transfer of learning.

Early At-Home Literacy

Cognitive theory argues that literacy development begins at birth. However, while some children discover the connection between sounds and letters early on through literacy experiences in the home, others do not. For these children, kindergarten provides the first formal instruction in early literacy activities. Often, this instruction must be direct, explicit, and systematic. A considerable amount of research supports such direct, explicit, and systematic reading instruction. Several studies compared different instructional programs, including direct phonics, embedded phonics, and context-emphasis approaches. In these studies, the direct instruction groups produced the greatest gains (Foorman et al. 1997). Honig (1996, p. 76) states that "effective skills instruction must be organized, sequenced, and comprehensive, while also being integrated with the overall English/language arts program, so that students practice and overlearn these skills until they are automatic." According to Moats (1998, p. 46), "systematic, explicit instruction leaves little to chance and thus ensures the success of most children."

In a balanced reading instruction model, children's early experiences with stories often include shared reading in which children may pretend to read the story, choral-read it with the teacher, or actually read it independently. It is important for teachers to model the reading process, encourage learners to actively participate in the process, and provide opportunities for them to be directly involved with the story. Shared reading provides learners with many experiences with story structure and broadens their knowledge of how stories are written. As students begin to encounter more sophisticated story structures, the teacher introduces story maps because children who did not have early at-home literacy experiences will not have internalized an awareness of story structure.

The Instructional Components of a Balanced Reading Approach

Figure 1.2 summarizes the eight instructional components of a balanced reading instruction approach.

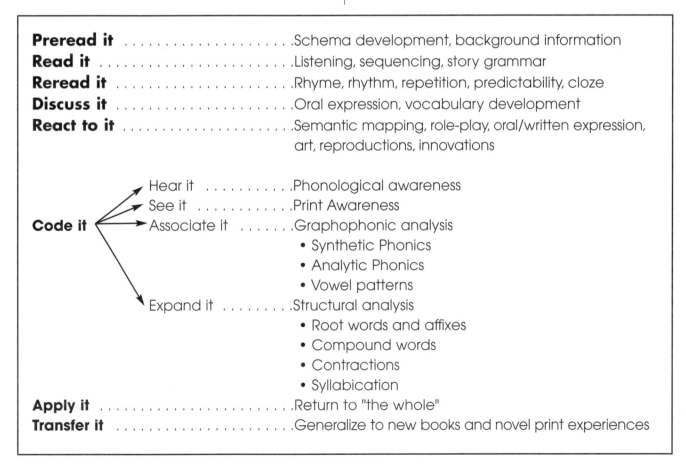

Figure 1.2 Instructional Components

Preread It

In this part of a balanced reading lesson, the emphasis is on the learner using prior knowledge to expand and relate more fully to the learning schema. Through discussion, the teacher helps children connect vocabulary and related concepts to their prior knowledge and experiences. In many cases, the teacher uses pictures in a Big Book to elicit the children's responses. The teacher often begins this discussion by focusing the students' attention on the cover of the book. The teacher may then draw a map or web on chart paper as the children provide information about the text. During this process of developing a semantic map, students have an opportunity to develop and expand their oral language. The concepts and words discussed during this part of the lesson provide the mental set that facilitates children's recognition of these words when they encounter them later in print. These activities provide teachers with an opportunity to "implant" language in preparation for the more visual aspects of reading that follow.

Read It

After the prereading activity has been completed, the teacher reads the story to the children. During this segment of the lesson, children listen to the story to enjoy it, but this listening experience also provides children with opportunities to develop the concept of story grammar. The teacher may assist the class in recognizing the beginning, middle, and end of the story.

Reread It

As the teacher rereads the story, she or he invites children to join in through choral reading. Rhyme, rhythm, and repetition facilitate this shared reading process for many children. During the rereading, the teacher points to the words as they are read, enabling the children to begin to associate what they *hear* with what they *see*. Effective shared reading stories contain predictable and easily recognizable language patterns. With repeated readings, the teacher may introduce a cloze activity, covering individual words with sticky notes and asking children to suggest replacement words that make sense (semantic cues) and sound right (syntactic cues). Each covered word is then uncovered to check for accuracy. Later, in a reading center, the teacher makes the Big Book available to the children so they can pretend to read or actually read it by themselves. This rereading may be done individually, in pairs, or in small peer groups.

Discuss It

After several readings, the teacher encourages further interaction with the text by asking open-ended questions designed to enhance students' understanding and encourage them to become personally involved. Questions should be based on story line and picture details in order to stimulate a variety of responses and engage children's thinking. Good questioning includes the following techniques:

- Encouraging open-ended responses: "How do you think he felt?"
- Accepting a variety of responses: "Are there any other ideas?"
- Guiding attention to detail in pictures: "Look at the bottom corner of the picture. What do you see?"
- Focusing attention on story line: "Can you find the main character?"
- Personalizing the story content: "What would you have done?"

Discussion questions that focus on learners' interaction with the story foster oral language expression, the immediate use of new vocabulary, and the development of new concepts.

React to It

When children are very familiar with the story content and have internalized the print, the teacher provides opportunities for them to react to it. This may be done through role-playing, chanting, singing, and drawing. Creating an innovation is another way to respond to a story. It is a more complex activity that needs to be practiced with the teacher. In creating an innovation, children make word substitutions that maintain a story's pattern or grammatic structure but change its meaning. Additional group responses may be encouraged through retelling the story, completing a story map or a story frame, or charting and illustrating a beginning-middle-end summary.

Code It

In a balanced reading model, the emphasis is on the development of skill learning that will transfer and generalize easily to other print situations. Therefore, the skill portion of the lesson is always introduced within the context of the story, chant, poem, or rhyme. The learner may practice the skill both in and out of context depending on the amount of direct instruction he or she needs. The phonics skill lesson could focus on any one or a combination of the following four literacy areas (see Figure 1.3):

- Phonological awareness
- Print awareness
- Graphophonic analysis
- Structural analysis

A more complete discussion of these four literacy areas, including suggested activities and strategies, is provided in chapters 3 through 6.

Apply It

After specific and direct instruction in selected skill areas, a return to "the whole" is necessary. In this segment of the lesson, emphasis is on providing practice within the context of familiar stories. For example, when rhyming words from a story are used in teaching phonological awareness, these words can then be emphasized as the story is reread. Such reinforcement of skills enables them to more easily transfer skills to novel print.

Transfer It

It is important that the teacher provide explicit and specific activities that enable children to transfer and generalize newly learned skills. This may be accomplished by providing many opportunities for learners to practice new skills with a variety of stories, songs, and chants. Thus, skills are taught directly in context, practiced when necessary out of context, applied to familiar text, and finally generalized to new stories and novel print.

The lesson plan format shown in Figure 1.4 may be used by teachers to plan this instructional process for implementation in the

Title:		
Process	**Materials**	**Activity**
Preread it		
Read it		
Reread it		
Discuss it		
React to it		
Code it		
Apply it		
Transfer it		

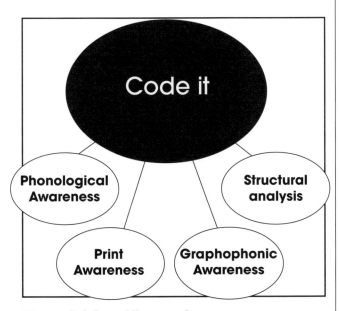

Figure 1.3 Four Literacy Areas

Figure 1.4 Lesson Plan Format

classroom. This lesson plan is an example of how a whole-to-part-to-whole philosophy of learning can be implemented with a variety of materials. Some published reading programs encourage the use of "decodable" texts, which are stories written with controlled linguistic vocabulary. We believe that this type of practice may be beneficial for some students who need more practice with a specific pattern or skill. Many children, however, find it easier to transfer learning when the story content is relevant to them personally and written in a style that is similar to their oral language. Therefore, skill instruction should include activities using a variety of texts.

Chapter 2

Focus on Phonics

To understand the components of a complete and balanced phonics program, it is important to be aware of several underlying processes that support the way children learn phonics. Phonics acquisition appears to occur in a systematic way that is both predictable and developmental. Learning phonics, therefore, is part of a developmental process, and students learn phonics most effectively when teachers understand the supportive processes underlying literacy.

Phonics Skill Acquisition Processes

One of the most critical precursors in reading and writing is oral language. In addition, auditory, visual, and tactile-kinesthetic perception provide equally important support (see Figure 2.1).

In the early years of a child's life, environment significantly influences literacy development. The extent to which a child encounters oral and written language in his or her environment affects the child's later mastery of phonics skills. Children who come to school with delays at the primary literacy level often experience listening and speaking problems which may be the result of difficulty with auditory processing. Related problems are manifested as these children progress to the level of secondary language acquisition, which involves reading and writing. Likewise, children with visual processing problems may have difficulty seeing differences among letters and words, making reading and writing difficult skills to acquire. Figure 2.2 illustrates the congruence between the two processes of language—oral (primary) and written (secondary).

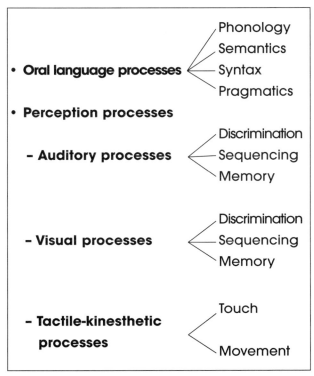

Figure 2.1 The Processes Supporting Literacy

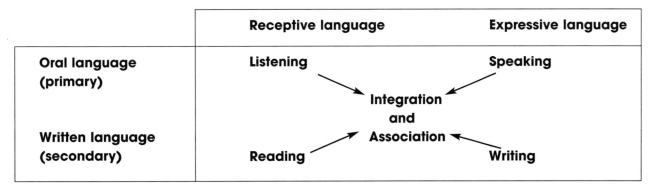

Figure 2.2 Language Processes

Approaches to Phonics Instruction

When either auditory or visual processing is inadequate or delayed developmentally, early instruction in oral language may be necessary. Phonics instruction in the past assumed that adequate primary language had been acquired; therefore, the various approaches to phonics instruction tackled this challenge with different levels of success. These approaches to phonics instruction are represented by stand-alone programs and basal programs.

Stand-Alone and Basal Phonics Programs

Traditionally, phonics curricula were published and sold as either stand-alone phonics programs or as part of basal programs. The stand-alone programs were usually synthetic in nature and were taught explicitly, with practice taking the form of workbook activities. Frequently, these programs were taught prior to reading and their focus skills were seen as prerequisites or "readiness" skills for reading.

The basal programs were similar to stand-alone programs in most respects, but treated phonics and comprehension as separate but parallel strands. Phonics skills were taught in isolation and apart from real stories. Most often, these programs placed heavy emphasis on synthetic phonics, using activities that were dependent on workbooks or skill-packs.

Although phonics skills were taught systematically and sequentially in both stand-alone and basal programs, there was little regard for meaningful context exhibited in instruction. With little or no connection to real stories or concepts, skills were rarely transferred to text and had to be retaught many times.

Balanced Phonics Instruction

In a balanced model of reading, phonics instruction has its foundation in real literature. This foundation may be accompanied by in-context and out-of-context practice. Repeated practice ensures greater fluency through increased automaticity of response. We recommend practice using repeated readings of familiar stories as well as of new stories and other print in the classroom. Instruction should also include implicit and explicit experiences and both auditory and visual strategies. Teachers should use the instructional process to assess individual needs and to build on individual children's learning strengths.

Reading Cueing Systems

As we have discussed, oral language and perception processes, support children's reading and writing. Fluent readers also rely on the following four cueing systems to read and write: (1) schema, (2) semantics, (3) syntax, and (4) graphophonics. Figure 2.3 shows the relationships among these four systems.

Schematic Cueing System

The schematic cueing system is largely based on the prior knowledge and experiences that the reader brings to reading. Most reading specialists agree that what the reader brings in terms of schema to the printed page is paramount to comprehension and allows the reader to go "beyond" what is stated on the page. Dechant (1993, p. 132) writes that "research and experience have amply demonstrated that the most important single factor influencing learning

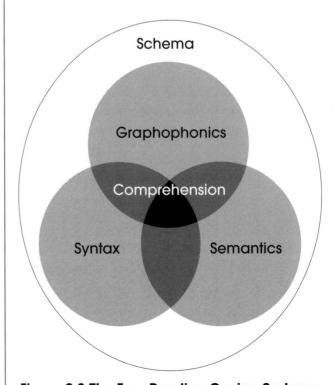

Figure 2.3 The Four Reading Cueing Systems

is what the learner already knows," referring to this knowledge as *within-mind cues* stored as part of the mind's schema. He explains that these schema, or within-mind cues, are the building blocks for the semantic context: "The semantic context takes on meaning because the reader is a virtual storehouse of past experiences" (p. 130).

Semantic and Syntactic Cueing Systems

Semantic and syntactic cues are frequently described as *within-text cues* and are most often found in the story or text itself. The semantic cueing system helps the reader look for meaning in words, sentences, paragraphs, and entire stories. The syntactic cueing system assigns meaning through grammatical structure and word order. These two cueing systems are components of the schematic cueing system in that they require activation of prior knowledge. With the schema cueing system activated, beginning readers often can figure out the meanings of words they don't know by recognizing similarities to known words; similarly, they can understand unfamiliar text by recognizing familiar structure and order in it. Beginning readers rely on context more than fluent readers do because they have not yet developed an arsenal of decoding strategies. Dechant (1993) describes the meaning cues children frequently use as including picture cues, lexical cues, semantic context (both within text and within mind), syntactic context, and morphemic cues (p. 148). Dechant also explains that when readers use context to predict a word, they are relatively reliable when making general predictions. However, specific predictions usually require an integration of meaning (semantic) cues with structural (syntactic) cues (pp. 146–147).

Graphophonic Cueing System

The graphophonic cueing system focuses on the visual representation of a word as a group or pattern of letters and their corresponding sounds. Good readers use such *within-word cues*, as Dechant calls them, in combination with the other three cueing systems to identify unfamiliar words. He also describes these within-word cues as configuration cues, graphemic cues, orthographic cues, phonological cues, graphophonemic cues, morphemic cues, and analogy cues (1993, p. 158).

Integration of All Language Processes in Instruction

All four cueing systems are important to reading fluency. Because children need access to a variety of reading cues, a balanced reading instruction program includes explicit and systematic instruction of all four major cueing systems. This provides learners with opportunities to make connections and more adequately store skills in long-term memory. Children who rely heavily on only one cueing system tend to be poor readers. Cunningham and Cunningham (1992) summarizes the relationship of brain-compatible instruction to reading and spelling acquisition. She identifies the following generalizations regarding successful readers:

- Fluent readers look at virtually all of the words and all of the letters in a word. This visual processing is extremely rapid because the brain expects certain letters to occur in sequence or patterns.

- Fluent readers usually recode words into sounds. They "think" the words in their minds using internal speech. They then check this phonological information with the visual information by analyzing the word for familiar spelling patterns. Saying the word helps the reader access meaning.

- Fluent readers recognize most words immediately and automatically without context. They process more than one cueing system simultaneously using context to determine if the word makes sense. The sequence appears to be that they identify the word first based on the pattern and then access its meaning.

- Fluent readers use spelling patterns and analogy to decode words.

- Fluent readers divide big words or "chunk" parts of words according to patterns stored in the brain through experience.

9

Cunningham goes on to explain how children learn to read words:

- Children from literate homes have over one thousand hours of informal reading and writing encounters before they come to school.

- Phonemic awareness is critical to success in beginning reading.

- Children who can decode well learn sight words better. In decoding a word, a child forms a phonological access route for that word in the memory bank.

- The division of a word into *onset* and *rime* is a psychological reality that supports the concept of highlighting word families. For example, in the word *Sam*, *S* is the onset and *am* is the rime. Children usually find it easier to divide syllables and words into their onsets (all letters before the vowel) and rimes (vowel and what follows). For example, it is easier to change *Sam* to *ham* than *Sam* to *sat*.

- Children who write become better readers.

While literature instruction and reading skills instruction are typically presented as separate programs, many educators believe that these components of language arts should be taught together (Fountas and Hannigan 1989; Heymsfeld 1989; Teale 1991). Dechant suggests that the traditional instructional dichotomy between literature and skills is a false one and that "skill teaching, strategy instruction, reciprocal teaching, and direct instruction can be personalized, contextualized, socialized, and interactive" (1993, p. 43). Routman states that "the reality is and always has been that phonics is part of whole language" (1996, p. 11). Trachtenburg (1990) recommends a whole-to-part-to-whole teaching approach that integrates phonics instruction with quality literature, explaining that "what is needed is an approach that combines the two in a complementary manner—a method that presents the two as mutually supportive—and [is] taught in a manner that makes the interrelationships clear to children. This approach is best achieved when phonics instruction is provided within the context of real reading tasks and texts,

especially through the use of quality children's literature" (p. 648). Honig (1996) also suggests that a literature-driven, language-rich reading program should be used in conjunction with a comprehensive, organized skill-development program.

Although some educators are suggesting that teachers use balanced reading instruction models, specific methods for implementation are lacking. As a result, few teachers have implemented such models. In *Literacy at the Crossroads*, Routman presents an outstanding analysis of the complex issues that have hindered the implementation of balanced reading programs in California and other states: "What happened in California is being called the 'failure of whole language.' It was not whole language that failed. It was the implementation of a set of practices without adequate funding, staff development, community support, and understanding" (1996, p. 22). While these factors may be partly to blame, the main problem is that the phonics portion of newer reading instruction models has not been given the attention it deserves in the instructional sequence. Reading programs must include phonics as an integral part of the instruction process. Dechant agrees, providing the following definition of reading:

Reading is an interactive process which begins as a top-down process, but almost simultaneously and in parallel moves back and forth between a top-down and bottom-up process.... [R]eading moves from whole to part to whole and when we focus on the parts we are implicitly talking about skill teaching. (1993, p. 42)

How Phonics Needs to Be Taught

As an integral part of a balanced reading instruction program, phonics instruction should meet the following criteria, drawn from research-based data:

- Phonics instruction should feature a whole-to-part-to-whole approach.

- Phonics instruction may need to be both implicit and explicit.

- Phonics instruction should contain both analytic and synthetic components.

- Phonics instruction should begin with real text and be practiced with real text; it may involve out-of-context practice; and it should provide for activities that encourage generalization and transfer to new text.
- Phonics instruction should be based on recent brain-compatible research and what is known about effective learning environments.
- Phonics instruction should include strategies that ultimately emphasize graphophonic analysis.
- Phonics instruction should include specific opportunities for transfer and generalization to other literature, as well as math, science, and social studies texts.

In addition to supporting reading, phonics instruction provides support for spelling and early writing experiences. Since phonics knowledge is fundamental to learning spelling, reading and spelling need to be taught in conjunction with one another rather than separately. Phonemic awareness begins to develop prior to children actually making sound-symbol associations and greatly influences early spelling development. In this early spelling process, children ask, "What word do I want to write? What sound do I hear in that word? What does it look like?" At this stage, children frequently look for visual models such as an alphabet poster in the room, and they may use one sound to represent a word. Children who have already acquired some sound-symbol associations tend to express themselves in a very free and flowing way, while children who are delayed in developing these associations are often frustrated as they try to represent their stories (talk) in print.

As auditory processing matures, the learning of phonics skills is facilitated. Gradually, children hear and write more sounds and letters. At first, children may select any vowel to insert in a word as they begin to develop awareness of vowels. Since long vowels are easier to hear than short vowels, they frequently appear earliest in the spelling process. (It should be noted that children who have auditory perceptual problems, particularly difficulty with auditory discrimination, will write whatever letters [graphemes] are associated with the sounds [phonemes] they hear. If a child hears *wabbit* for *rabbit*, he or she will probably spell *rabbit* with a *w*. If a child hears *thumb* as *fum*, she or he will probably write it as *f*, *fm*, or *fum*.)

When children begin to associate the sounds they hear with letters, they feel more empowered to write. As they progress through early developmental spelling stages, their increased ability to use phoneme-grapheme associations facilitates their spelling acquisition. Children make the transition from auditory to visual spelling when their reading of real words has expanded, and they rely on perception of visual patterns to make judgments about spelling. When confronted with words that they have not yet stored as visual patterns, however, children at this level of development often return to an auditory strategy, asking, "What do I hear in _____? What letter is that?" Thus, it is not unusual to see developmental spellers using a mix of auditory and visual strategies. For children who get "stuck" at an auditory level, teachers need to do some guided writing that emphasizes the visual patterns of spelling.

Chapter 3

Phonological Awareness: Hear It

As discussed previously, literacy is developmental in nature and dependent on the integrity of several sensory and perceptual processes. The three major processes that influence emergent literacy are (1) oral language development, (2) auditory processes, and (3) visual processes (see Figure 2.1).

Oral Language and Auditory Processing

Oral language development and auditory processing precede visual processing. They are vital to the acquisition of later literacy skills. *Oral language* consists of the following components:

1. phonemes (sounds),
2. semantics (meaning),
3. syntax (grammar and word order), and
4. pragmatics (the social context of language).

Auditory processing refers to the ability to both hear language and understand it. The specific sensory and perceptual components of auditory processing include

1. discrimination,
2. sequencing, and
3. memory.

Although oral language development and auditory processing are crucial to emerging literacy, parents may be unaware of their importance and may not foster or monitor this development. Even when language or auditory processing problems are identified early by a speech pathologist or psychologist, the results are rarely shared with teachers, and early intervention opportunities are thus missed. Early attention to a child's language development is critical and can prevent failure at higher literacy levels.

Listening and speaking are the first steps in acquiring language. Parents and other family members often have the greatest impact on this level of literacy development, since most children learn to listen and speak before they are of school age. In this primary phase, auditory processing is very important and can significantly influence language learning. This is the time when young children begin to master the phonological (sound), semantic (meaning), and syntactic (order) components of language. As children begin to recognize print and identify its role in their environment, they enter the secondary phase of language acquisition. While the secondary phase is dependent on the primary phase, the emphasis changes from sound awareness to visual awareness. In the secondary language acquisition phase, visual processing emerges and functions simultaneously with auditory processing. With more fluency and automaticity of reading, visual processing becomes increasingly important.

The idea that reading and writing are based in oral language is not new; however, this aspect of literacy learning is often ignored by educators because children are assumed to have developed oral language and auditory skills prior to entering school. Recent research strongly suggests that instruction in auditory processing and oral language can facilitate early literacy learning.

Figure 3.1 further delineates the close relationship between the primary oral language phase and the secondary reading and writing, or visual, phase. Both phases focus on syntax and semantics, with the secondary phase shifting its emphasis from phonological awareness (sound) to graphophonic awareness (visual).

Phonological Awareness

One of the most important components of oral language development is phonological awareness. Cunningham (1995, p. 10) defines phonological awareness as the ability to manipulate sounds. Tunmer and Chapman (1996) defines it as the recognition that "a spoken word consists of a sequence of individual

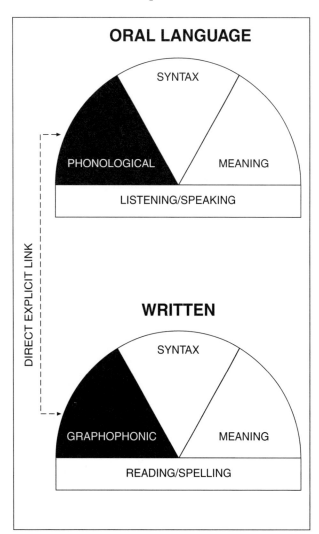

Figure 3.1 The Relationship Between Oral and Written Language

sounds." Adams (1990, pp. 209–210) extends this definition by suggesting that phonological awareness involves the knowledge that syllables and words can be divided into a relatively small set of sounds (phonemes) that in turn correspond to graphemes. It is not unusual for educators to use the term *phonological awareness* as a synonym for *phonemic awareness*, but the terms mean two different things. Phonological awareness is a broader term that refers to many different auditory components of language. Phonemic awareness is part of phonological awareness and specifically refers to the ability to hear and manipulate the sounds of language.

Reading Success and Phonological Awareness

Phonological awareness appears to be the strongest single determinant of the success a child will have in learning to read (Stanovich 1986). Early research by Calfee, Lindamood, and Lindamood (1973, pp. 293–298) found that the ability to manipulate phonetic components of spoken language is predictive of success in reading and spelling, and that, in fact, students' ability to attend to and manipulate phonemes strongly correlates with their reading success all the way through twelfth grade. In a more recent publication on the Lindamood Program, Truch (1998, p. 10) states, "it is abundantly clear from the nearly thirty years of research that good decoding depends on a high level of phonological awareness and that reading disabilities are caused by underlying difficulties in phonological processing." Dechant (1993, pp. 229–231) states that phonological processing is very important to the development of language and speech because it is significantly related to the development of auditory discrimination, analysis, and synthesis, as well as articulation and auditory sequential memory. It appears that children who lack phonological awareness have difficulty compensating with visual skills. Research shows that reading success requires the development of auditory *and* visual processing skills.

When Phonological Awareness Develops

While most educators agree that phonological awareness is a component of reading success, there is some controversy as to whether phonological awareness develops before learning to read or as a result of learning to read. Adams (1990, pp. 209–210) suggests that phonological awareness occurs prior to phonics instruction and is "an insight, an understanding," not a skill acquired through drill. Byrne and Fielding-Barnsley (1991, p. 451) agree that phonological awareness is best fostered through connection to real literature. According to Dechant (1993, p. 227), phonological and phonemic awareness develop earlier than print awareness. Tunmer and Chapman (1996, p. 105) suggests that phonemic awareness is a "developmentally distinct kind of linguistic functioning that develops separately from and later than basic speaking and listening." A study by Lundberg, Frost, and Peterson (1988, p. 263) concluded that preschool (prereading) training in phonological awareness can have a facilitating effect on the subsequent acquisition of reading and spelling. They conducted their research in Denmark, where children do not start school until they are seven years old and where phonological awareness training is not done prior to reading instruction. The researchers' conclusions were that phonological awareness developed outside the context of the alphabetic system with explicit instruction and facilitated more successful reading and spelling among students through the second grade.

Byrne and Fielding-Barnsley (1991, p. 451) concluded that phonological awareness and letter knowledge are necessary but not sufficient for the acquisition of sound-letter association, also known as the *alphabetic principle:* "Mere knowledge of phonemic organization can apparently be supplemented by instruction in how to use the knowledge."

Dechant's Model of Phonological Awareness

Authors such as Adams (1990), Dechant (1993), and Torgeson (1998) have identified slightly different levels of phonological awareness, but most identify rhyming, segmenting, and blending as important components. Dechant also describes levels of phonemic awareness and suggests that there are different tasks that can be learned at various developmental levels. Ehri (1989) suggests that phonological awareness includes elements of phonemic segmentation, blending sequences of separately articulated phonemes to form a syllable or word, detecting rhyming and alliteration, and manipulating, deleting, or substituting phonemes in words (see Figure 3.2).

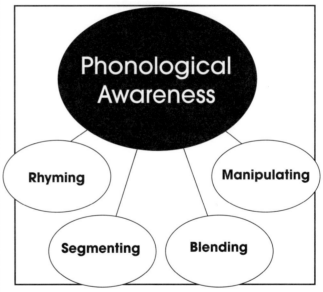

Figure 3.2 Components of Phonological Awareness

Dechant (1993, p. 231) defines three main levels of phonological awareness, as represented in Figure 3.3. This model is the basis for both the assessments and the lesson plans in Part 2 of this book. We recommend that teachers use this model as a guideline for both instruction and assessment because it enables teachers to identify developmental levels and sequence their instruction to match children's learning progress.

The first level of phonological awareness is the most basic and general stage. At this level, children become aware of gross differences among sounds, hearing words as separate entities, for example. They also become aware of rhyme, distinguishing words that sound alike, and begin to segment words into syllables, identifying how many parts there are in a word.

After considerable learning at the first level, children advance to the second level, shifting their focus from the general features of language to more specific details, including specific consonant sounds, words that start with the same sound, and alliteration. They also become aware of onsets and rimes and can separate initial consonant sounds from rhyming sounds, by segmenting *mat* into /*m*/ and /*at*/, for example.

Moving to level three requires the successful acquisition of the skills in the previous two levels and more complicated auditory process-

ing. At this highest level of phonological awareness, children segment words into individual sounds, blend individual phonemes to make words, and manipulate words by making additions, deletions, and/or substitutions of vowels and consonants.

Other Models of Phonological Awareness

There are some other models that can be useful in structuring phonological instruction and assessment. Adams (1990) identifies the following levels of phonemic awareness, which are listed from simple to complex:

1. Nursery-rhyme level
2. Oddity task level (onset and rhyme)
3. Blending level
4. Phonemic segmentation level
5. Phonemic manipulation level

Robertson and Salter (1995b) wrote a test designed to assess phonemic awareness called *The Phonological Awareness Test*, published by

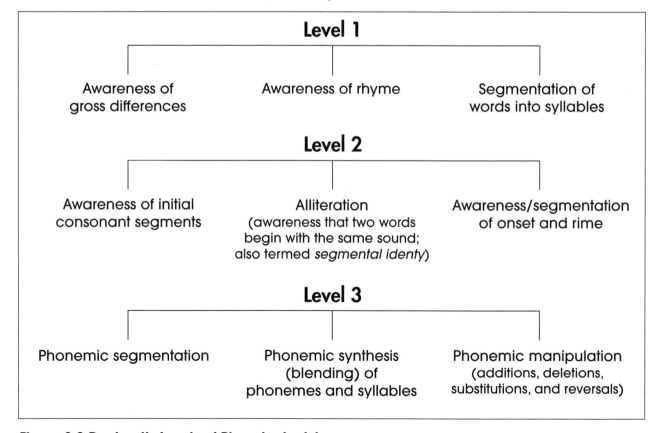

Figure 3.3 Dechant's Levels of Phonological Awareness

LinguiSystems. This test assesses students' ability to rhyme, segment, isolate phonemes, delete, substitute, blend, identify graphemes, and decode various made-up words (pseudowords) representing visual patterns. The test provides very specific diagnostic information for teachers regarding students' phonological processing abilities. Torgeson and Bryant (1994) wrote the *Test of Phonological Awareness*, which is sold in two versions, one for kindergartners and one for the early elementary grades.

Articles published by Griffith and Olsen (1992) and Yopp (1992) provide numerous classroom activities to encourage the development of phonological awareness. Programs such as *The Phonological Awareness Kit* (Robertson and Salter 1995a) and *Phonological Awareness Training for Reading* (Torgesen and Bryant 1993) also present lessons for use with young children.

Our preference is that teachers use stories or storylike materials with lessons, supporting the view that phonological awareness is an insight rather than a skill acquired by drill and exercise. According to Adams's model (1990), the development of phonological awareness needs to occur in the context of real literature. Reading stories provides students with opportunities to hear phonemes and see their visual match in print. Print awareness also is developed most effectively in the context of real literature, particularly when children are beginning to perceive the relationship between speech and print.

The Logical Transition from Sound to Print

Because oral language occurs before written language, teaching language sounds before teaching the letters that represent the sounds is developmentally appropriate. Recent research supports beginning with instruction of the target sound and then making the connection to the abstract symbol, or letter, that represents that sound (Lindamood and Lindamood 1998; McGuinness, McGuinness, and Donohue 1995; Moats 1998). Moats makes the point simply: "Alphabetic writing was invented to represent speech; speech was not learned from reading.

We should teach awareness of the sound system (phonology) and anchor letters to it" (1998, p. 45).

In a study involving first-grade children, McGuinness, McGuinness, and Donohue discovered that early phonological processing skills and reading are interrelated and that "phoneme awareness must be connected in a coherent way to graphemes...to grasp the logic of the alphabet principle and learn accurate and fluent decoding skills" (1995, p. 851). Routman (1991, pp. 148–149) says that "children naturally go from sound to letter, from the oral mode to the written mode, when writing and using temporary spelling. Going from sound to letter respects the principle that learning proceeds from the known to the unknown."

McGuinness, McGuinness, and Donahue (1995, p. 843) affirm the need to move from sound to print, suggesting that an alphabet is a code for the phonemic units of speech: "All writing systems, including alphabets, are transcriptions of conversations or potential conversations. Thus, they only make sense (are logical) when they are taught the right way around, that is, from sound to print." They reject reading programs that violate this principle: "The first to go is phonics, which teaches the alphabet principle backwards, from print to sound." They conclude that, while phonological processing is necessary for learning to read, it should be taught *in conjunction with* the alphabetic principle and the phoneme-grapheme association.

Concepts of print usually develop simultaneously with phonological awareness in a language-rich and print-rich classroom environment. Most children who enter school without adequate experiences with oral language profit from emerging literacy teaching strategies that include phonological experiences. These experiences can easily be developed with materials already available in most prekindergarten and kindergarten classrooms. Nursery rhymes are the easiest materials to use and are popular in early-childhood classrooms. In addition, Big Books used for shared reading are already a part of classroom libraries and can easily facilitate activities to build phonological awareness.

Children at Risk for Not Developing Phonological Awareness

There are three main populations of children who are at risk for failing to develop sufficient phonological awareness. The first group of at-risk learners are children who are delayed in acquiring their first language. This delay could be in phonology, syntax, semantics, and/or pragmatics. A second group of at-risk learners consists of children who enter school with an oral dialect different from the one they will read and write. Such children may be "bidialectic" prior to entering school. The third group of at-risk children are speakers of English as a second language. Such learners are typically unfamiliar with the phonological and phonemic features of English. For such at-risk students, direct, explicit instruction in phonological awareness is crucial in prekindergarten and kindergarten. It is important that these students receive this instruction before formal phonics is introduced.

In many prekindergarten and kindergarten classrooms, there is a wide range of students' abilities. A recent position statement by the International Reading Association and the National Association for the Education of Young Children reported that teachers throughout the United States are teaching increasingly diverse student populations:

> Kindergarten classes now include children who are participating for the first time in an organized early childhood program....Children in the group may speak different languages at varying levels of proficiency. Because of these individual and experiential variations, it is common to find within a kindergarten classroom a five-year range in children's literacy-related skill and functioning. (International Reading Association 1998)

If a child enters kindergarten hearing sounds incorrectly, we may still understand the speech approximations and respond to the message. This is consistently the pattern shown by most adults as they respond to children learning to speak. As early as eighteen to twenty-four months of age, infants vocalize utterances that may, in fact, differ almost completely from the conventions of the home language. However, if adults understand the message, they generally respond to its meaning (semantics), not to its linguistic correctness. With maturation, children focus more and more attention on the parts of language. At approximately eighteen to twenty-four months of age, they begin to chunk two words together. As the length of children's early utterances increases, children become increasingly focused on word order (syntax). As children's vocabulary and sentence length continue to increase, they become more aware of the "correctness" of phoneme production, or articulation.

By the time they start school, most children have acquired and integrated an awareness of correct phoneme production, word order, and meaning. However, since there is great variation among children in normal oral language development and since circumstances place some children at risk, children entering school should be assessed on their oral language skills, including the areas of semantics, syntax, and phonology. Children who cannot hear the differences between short vowels or who delete, substitute, or distort individual phonemes may have auditory processing problems that can interfere with literacy development by hindering phonological awareness. These auditory problems can also interfere with the development of higher-level skills such as those needed to make phoneme-grapheme associations. These associations are essential in learning synthetic phonics and spelling. Teachers assessing the stages of developmental spelling will notice a one-to-one correlation between the spelling stages and children's ability to hear sounds, associate them with appropriate letters, and apply this ability to writing.

Torgesen, Wagner, and Rashotte (1994, p. 285) suggest that phonological awareness training should be included for children who are at risk or who have been identified as having reading disabilities. They suggest that training for these children needs to be both explicit and intense.

Teaching Suggestions

Since phonological processing is believed to precede print awareness, the following suggestions are concerned primarily with auditory processing. For instruction with an emphasis on auditory processing, well-known nursery rhymes provide a strong basis upon which to develop skill lessons. In addition, Big Books that develop a sense of rhyme, rhythm, and repetition are particularly effective. You may wish to alter and/or expand the suggestions provided here. You will find in Appendix 2 the full or partial texts for *Jack and Jill, Little Boy Blue, Annabel, Down by the Bay, The Little Yellow Chicken, My Wonderful Aunt, The Number Cruncher,* and *Time Warp,* which are the texts that serve as a basis for the lesson plans in Part 2.

Using the basic lesson plan shown in Figure 1.4, begin your lesson by reading the literature aloud. If you read the nursery rhyme *Jack and Jill,* for example, you might include activities such as discussing the pictures, listening to the rhyme, choral-reading with the children, and using the text or pictures for a follow-up discussion. After activities like these, it is appropriate to use the story for skill instruction. Here are some possible activities based on the phonological awareness levels outlined in Figure 3.3:

- Awareness of gross differences: identifying words, such as *Jack* and *Jill.*
- Awareness of rhyme: listening for words that rhyme, such as *Jill* and *hill* or *down* and *crown.*
- Segmenting words into syllables: listening for one- and two-syllable words, such as *fetch* and *water.*
- Awareness of initial consonant segments: brainstorming words that begin with the same sound; finding pictures of words beginning with this sound and pasting them on a wall chart.
- Awareness of alliteration: using words that begin with the same sound to make alliterative sentences:

  Jolly Jack and Jill jumped in the jello.

  Jack and Jill juggled juicy lemons in the jungle.

- Awareness and segmentation of onsets and rimes: brainstorming words that rhyme with *Jill* and *hill,* such as *pill, mill, sill, fill, bill,* and *will,* and then segmenting the words into onsets and rimes:

Onset	Rime
J-	-ill
h-	-ill
p-	-ill
m-	-ill
s-	-ill
f-	-ill
b-	-ill
w-	-ill

- Phonemic segmentation: separating phonemes in commonly used words (a good way to do this is to use colored tiles on an overhead projector to help children visualize whole words and word parts):

  /J/ /a/ /ck/
  /J/ /i/ /ll/
  /u/ /p/
  /f/ /e/ /ll/
  /d/ /ow/ /n/
  /w/ /e/ /n/ /t/
  /a/ /f/ /t/ /er/

- Phonemic blending: using colored tiles to blend segmented words back together and then saying the whole word.
- Phonemic manipulation: changing the initial sound of rhyming words (changing *pill* to *mill,* or *hill* to *sill);* manipulating words and word segments with colored tiles:

  Jill (use four tiles with same color)
  hill (substitute different color for first letter)

Specific prototype lesson plans for each of these activities are provided in Part 2. These lessons use both nursery rhymes and shared reading books. They include materials appropriate for use with children at the early emergent, upper emergent, early fluency, and fluency levels of development as well as materials for struggling readers at the intermediate grade level.

Chapter 4

Print Awareness: See It

In addition to developing phonological awareness, children must also develop print awareness in the early phases of literacy development. According to Dechant (1993, p. 244), print awareness is a type of metalinguistic understanding that includes the knowledge that writing is composed of letters and moves (in English) from left to right; that words are separated by spaces and can represent speech, objects, or meaning; and that sentences can tell a story. Marie Clay (1991) is well known for her early work in developing assessments to measure children's knowledge of print concepts. The Concepts of Print Checklist shown in Figure 4.1 (and provided as a reproducible in part 2 of this book) can be used as a guide for the development of those visual components most important to the beginning reading process.

How Children Develop Print Awareness

Dechant suggests that, as with phonological awareness, direct instruction is usually necessary for children to develop print awareness. Although some children learn to identify letters before they enter school, usually as a result of being raised in print-rich environments, literacy does not generally "naturally blossom forth by simple exposure" (Adams 1990, p. 210). Children develop print awareness best by being read to, reading to themselves, or reading along in a shared-book experience. (Books used for shared reading should be predictable and should contain rhyme, rhythm, and a repetitive pattern.) Singing and/or chanting also provide opportunities to experience the print patterns of letters, syllables, words, and sentences.

Awareness of Print-Speech Correspondence

For young children to use print awareness for reading purposes, they must first understand that print corresponds directly with speech and the sounds of words. Sometimes children have difficulty acquiring print awareness because of developmental delays in visual processing. There are many features in a word that are necessary to track. Adams (1990, p. 112) states that "the speed and accuracy with which young readers can recognize individual letters is a critical determinant for their reading proficiency and future growth." Dechant (1991) presents very detailed guidelines for teaching letters, including suggestions for determining the best sequence of letter recognition, how to emphasize differences rather than similarities in letters, and letter-orientation activities to assist learners with easily confused letters such as *b* and *d*.

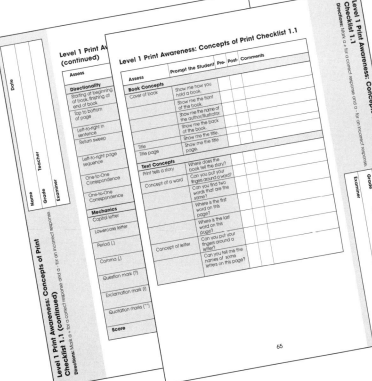

Figure 4.1 Concepts of Print Checklist

Sound-Symbol Associations

Once children develop adequate awareness of phonological and print elements of reading, they are ready to make sound-symbol associations, which are important phonics cues in reading and spelling. This awareness of sound-symbol associations is an "enabling skill" that will not in and of itself enable children to begin to read. Bradley and Bryant (1983) caution that teaching children to recognize letters or sounds separate from one another produces little or no benefit to reading but that teaching them jointly does facilitate learning to read. Dechant (1993, p. 256) supports this view and summarizes his chapter on phonological and print awareness by stating that neither skill area is adequate by itself: "They are important enabling skills, but must lead to a mastery of grapheme-phoneme correspondences.…Children, if they are to learn to read, must learn how print tracks speech (including the phonemes) and meaning, and it does not come naturally." This making of associations between sounds and symbols requires greater higher-order thinking, or cognitive ability, than does recognizing a sound or letter.

The process of associating sounds and symbols is especially difficult in English because its rules are not completely regular. There are twenty-six letters in the English alphabet. Considering, however, that there are both uppercase and lowercase letters, children must learn to identify and form fifty-two letters, or graphemes. Reutzel and Cooter (1996, p. 289) cite research that supports letter knowledge as the single best predictor of first-grade reading ability. They concluded that the key question in building a balanced reading program is not whether one should teach phonics, but which phonics generalizations are most important to teach and how they should be taught (p. 249).

Word Recognition and Comprehension

Children continue to develop skills in phonological and print awareness as they progress through the various stages of word recognition and comprehension in the process of becoming fluent readers. It is becoming increasingly apparent to educators that children in the beginning-to-read process use phonological and print cues differently than experienced readers do. Beginning readers rely on context and environmental cues, while experienced readers use a wider variety of cueing systems to identify word shape, word length, word configuration, and specific letters. As children become more aware of patterns or chunks in words, they begin to recognize words more automatically because they store them in visual memory.

Beginning readers must be able to remember and identify the unique features of individual letters in order to progress successfully. Children appear to develop letter identification and discrimination initially by attending to letter shapes. When identifying words, beginning readers sometimes look only at the first letter and then guess the word. Through encountering more opportunities to decode words, early readers develop the ability to predict letter patterns in words. Like a computer, the brain becomes a pattern detector, using visual processing instead of auditory processing or syntactic processing to identify words. The fact that the brain is a pattern detector is reason to teach word patterns such as onsets and rimes, root words and affixes, syllabication, and so on. When children are taught various within-word patterns, they are able to apply these patterns to unknown words.

Relevant and predictable patterns, not rules, assist beginning readers. According to Moats (1998, p. 47), "awareness and use of organizational patterns, not memorization of rules, facilitates learning; the goal of insight is to read more fluently, not to recite orthographic trivia." Wylie and Durrell (1970) discovered that about 500 primary-grade words are derived from only thirty-seven phonograms (rimes). Recent research continues to support the importance of teaching rimes to beginning readers, confirming the fact that children use the onset-rime strategy to make letter-sound associations (Adams 1990, Goswami and Mead 1992, Moustafa 1997). In discussing specific vowel patterns, May explains that "the prediction power of the five patterns ranges from 77 percent to 89 percent, each of which is much better than predictions on the basis of chance alone. Teaching children vowel (syllable) patterns can make a difference in their fluency and comprehension" (1998, p. 194).

Just and Carpenter (1987, p. 329) have found that skilled readers decode words more by looking at their distinctive graphemes than by noticing their overall shapes. Dechant (1993, p. 159) suggests that grapheme knowledge is specific to letters that make up a word. Generally, children identify words by focusing first on the initial letter, then on the final letter, then on the medial letters, and finally on letter clusters. Dechant explains that "the orthography of a word is significant because it maps onto the phonology of the word." Put another way, the written form of a word is significant because it represents the sound of the word.

Recoding

Gagne, Yekovich, and Yekovich (1993, p. 283) provide additional information with respect to the interrelatedness of auditory and visual aspects of reading: "By far the most research on differences between skilled and less skilled readers has focused on the recoding process." They state that evidence strongly supports the theory that skilled readers perform recoding faster and more easily than beginning readers do. Just and Carpenter (1987, p. 93) define *recoding* as "the process of converting a visually based representation into a speech code." This means that when a reader sees a word, the visual image immediately moves to the auditory processing part of the brain. If the meaning of the word is part of the reader's oral vocabulary, he or she will transfer that meaning to the written word as well. If the word is not in his or her oral vocabulary, he or she will decode the word without knowing its meaning. It is important for teachers to be aware of oral versus written vocabularies when assessing students' reading comprehension. It may seem that young readers are able to identify words correctly if they can pronounce them, but research has shown that this may not be so.

Just and Carpenter (1987, p. 93) support the idea that, since beginning readers know spoken language, they may use a speech code to help themselves learn to read. Beginning readers seem to rely on this form of recoding more than experienced readers do. Just and Carpenter see the recoding process as having two phases: prelexical and postlexical. In the *prelexical phase*, a beginning reader sounds out a word and then uses its oral form to access its meaning. In the *postlexical phase*, access to meaning becomes more visual, making the prelexical speech code superfluous.

Other Word-Identification Processes

Ehri (1997) describes two similar word-identification processes. She explains that one decoding process requires matching. When readers match a printed word with a known pattern, their long-term memory is activated and they are able to access meaning. The other process is a kind of recoding in which a printed word is translated into a sound pattern, which in turn activates word meaning:

1. The reader separates the unfamiliar or lengthy word into syllables.
2. The reader generates the sound patterns in each syllable.
3. The reader strings the sounds together.
4. The reader uses the sounds to activate memory and access the word's meaning.

Ehri concludes that readers require knowledge of phonemes (sounds), syllables (word parts), and morphemes (word parts that contain meaning).

Early Spelling

As in the process of learning to speak, in which children initially articulate parts of words and sentences, early spelling involves a whole-to-part progression. Beginning writers often tell their stories in pictures. Later, they may use one letter to represent a word. Eventually, they will begin to add more parts until they are producing entire words. Once a word is established as a pattern in the writer's visual memory, there is no longer a need to sound out. However, when a young writer comes to a word that has not yet been stored as a visual pattern, she or he will revert to using a sound-by-sound, letter-by-letter association process.

The Cueing Systems

Good readers use a variety of cueing systems as they tackle unknown words. Word-recognition strategies must not be limited to any one cueing system, and skills should be taught in conjunction with schematic (in-mind) cues, syntactic (in-text) cues, and semantic (within-word) cues.

Dechant explains the syntactic cueing system this way: "The syntactic cue system, commonly referred to as the syntactic context, is another important aid in predicting oneself through print....Readers do a better job of comprehending if they can process language structures or the patterned regularities among the elements of the sentence" (1993, p. 153). Dechant refers to these elements as *interword* cues; they include word order, function words, and punctuation (1993, p. 154). Just and Carpenter (1987, p. 137) identify the following additional syntactic interword cues:

- patterns of word order
- word class (i.e., noun, verb)
- intonation patterns
- structure or function words
- affixes
- redundancy cues

The fluent reader is able to recognize syntactic cues more easily when teachers specifically draw attention to them as they appear in text during shared and guided reading.

Dechant (1993, p. 158) also describes a number of within-word cues used by good readers to decode unknown words. These within-word cues include graphemes (letters), orthographic elements (spelling patterns), phonological elements (sounds), grapho-phonemes (sound-symbol associations), morphemes (meaningful word parts), and analogic elements (familiar patterns). Again, the best learning experiences for children occur when all of these features are observed and focused on in the context of real literature, as opposed to being practiced in isolated exercises.

Teaching Suggestions

Children who have not developed a consistent pattern for reproducing a letter and children experiencing orientation and discrimination problems need direct instruction. Visual perceptual problems involving discrimination and spatial orientation further complicate the development of print awareness, including grapheme identification and written reproductions. Practice should be embedded in real print materials. These children may need considerable practice before skills become automatic.

Dechant (1993, p. 249) summarizes his research (1991) and that of others concerning letter discrimination instruction as follows:

- Teach capital letters before lowercase letters.
- Present letters in the order of difficulty.
- Note differences rather than similarities.
- Use color coding to call attention to individual letters in a word.
- Use color to highlight critical features of individual letters.
- Use transparencies to help show letter differences.
- Use kinesthetic teaching techniques (tracing and copying).
- Highlight the salient features of letters.
- Match letters to their duplicates in different words.
- Find letters from memory.

What follows are specific strategies for teaching print awareness including recognition and identification of letters, awareness of environmental print, and concepts regarding words (see Figure 4.2).

Awareness of Environmental Print

Specific print awareness skill lessons should be developed in conjunction with the use of materials such as Big Books, poetry, nursery rhymes, environmental print, and print displays on classroom walls and bulletin boards. Teachers can use the following activities to provide children with meaningful print experiences:

- Collect examples of environmental print to display on chart paper. These examples could include print from street signs, maps, restaurants, cereal boxes, and so on.

- Make a classroom alphabet frieze using environmental print.

- Make a classroom alphabet frieze using children's names. (You can use other names of people in the school community for any letters not appearing in class members' names.)

- Using magnetic boards and letters, have children find all the letters that are the same (categorizing and classifying).

- Provide manipulative activities for tracing individual letters of the alphabet. (See specific tracing suggestions earlier in this section.)

- Using phonological awareness lessons that resulted in charts of pictures beginning with the same sound, label each picture and highlight the initial letter.

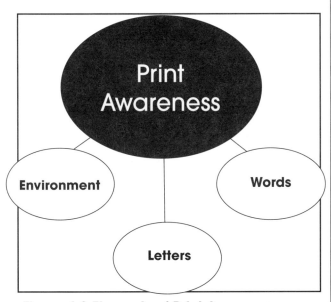

Figure 4.2 Elements of Print Awareness

Recognition and Identification of Letters

Tracing activities can help children learn to identify letters, develop correct left-to-right motion, and improve handwriting. Children can trace letters projected on the chalkboard with an overhead projector. Other multisensory tracing experiences include tracing letters made of various textures or writing letters in shaving cream or in a sand or rice tray. Here are some other possible activities:

- Create manipulative centers where children can trace, match, locate, and form letters and words in a multisensory approach, including the visual, auditory, kinesthetic, and tactile modalities. Materials may include clay, shaving cream, colored glue, gel in plastic baggies, screens and wax crayons, alphabet tiles (magnetic or plastic letters), transparencies for use with an overhead projector, color-highlight tape or highlighters, and sand, rice, salt, or cornmeal trays lined with colored paper.

- Color-code letters from a familiar text.

Concepts Regarding Words

The following activities will help children develop some key print awareness concepts involving entire words:

- Using rhyming words from phonological awareness lessons, develop word-family charts. Highlight onsets in one color and rimes in another.

- Using word-family charts, write sentences with alliteration, color coding the first letter of each word.

- Develop a word wall of irregular words.

- Have children search through a page from a story for a particular letter or word.

The skills outlined in the Concepts of Print Checklist (see Figure 4.1) should be taught in the context of Big Book shared reading lessons. See Part 2 of this book for specific prototype lesson plans for teaching print awareness skills.

Chapter 5

Graphophonic Analysis: Associate It

This chapter focuses on the relationship between sounds and the letters or letter combinations that are used to represent those sounds in the English language. The letter-sound relationship, or the way speech directly matches print, is known as the *alphabetic principle* or *alphabetic code*. The instructional approach used to teach the alphabetic principle is commonly known as *phonics*, or *graphophonic analysis*. In graphophonic analysis, a reader looks at a word consisting of a variety of letters and letter combinations and translates that visual image into speech sounds. Graphophonic analysis also involves looking at certain patterns within words and analyzing their sounds based on the position of the patterns within the words. Phonological awareness and print awareness (discussed in chapters 3 and 4, respectively) provide the foundation for phonics instruction.

The Importance of Phonics Instruction

Phonics instruction is a means to an end; that is, a vital tool that makes reading comprehension possible. Dechant explains just how vital it is:

> Teaching of phonics, or the grapheme-phoneme correspondences, is what leads to automatic semantic activation, to internalization of the alphabetic principle, to proficiency in word identification, to better prediction in reading, and ultimately to better comprehension....Phonics instruction develops the understanding that the letters of words mimic the phonemic sequences of spoken words. (1993, pp. 342–343)

Traditionally, phonics was taught in isolation. In contrast, a balanced early literacy program includes direct phonics instruction that

- follows a whole-to-part-to-whole process;
- occurs in a meaningful context;
- is related to schema;
- proceeds from the known to the unknown;
- is related to semantic and syntactic cueing systems;
- is related to phonological and print awareness;
- is based on visual patterns; and
- can be generalized.

Some children have the ability to decipher the alphabetic code implicitly and learn to read—there is always a small percentage of children who either come to school already reading or who will learn to read regardless of their formal instruction. Others experience some level of difficulty and require more explicit, direct, and systematic instruction. These students also need contextual practice before they can decode accurately and fluently. Even if children are able to use semantic and syntactic cues appropriately, their decoding may be erratic if they have not acquired the alphabetic principle.

Graphophonic Analysis

Formal reading instruction of the alphabetic principle proceeds from print (graphemes) to sound (phonemes)—hence the term *graphophonic*. There are three approaches to teaching the alphabetic principle: synthetic phonics, analytic phonics, and vowel patterns. These approaches may be conceptualized as the graphophonic triad, shown in Figure 5.1.

Synthetic Phonics

Synthetic phonics is part of the graphophonic triad of phonics instruction. It is a teaching approach that introduces children to individual grapheme-phoneme correspondences before teaching them how to blend letters and letter chunks to form syllables or whole words. To learn the word *cat*, for example, children first learn that *c* = /k/, *a* = /a/, and *t* = /t/. Then they blend the sounds together to form the whole word. For some children, especially those with weak phonological and/or print awareness abilities, this is a most difficult task.

Synthetic phonics programs include

- an emphasis on part-to-whole learning;
- mostly out-of-context practice;
- a dependence on phonological and print awareness;
- an emphasis on auditory processing, including discrimination, sequencing, memory, and blending;

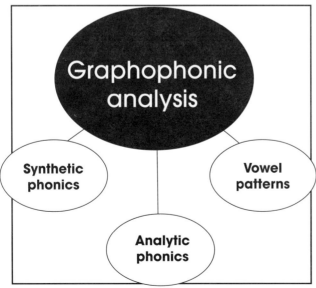

Figure 5.1 Elements of Graphophonic Analysis

- a combination of explicit and implicit phonics instruction;
- practice with decodable text; and
- dictation (spelling) practice.

Synthetic phonics is a very important part of beginning spelling and writing instruction. Making the sound-to-symbol connection helps the beginning writer get her or his thoughts on paper. As Routman explains:

> [C]hildren naturally go from sound to letter, from the oral mode to the written mode, when writing and using invented spelling. Going from sound to letter respects the principle that learning proceeds from the known to the unknown. When children start with real words and what they know, they can hold the sound and connect it to a letter in their minds. (1991, pp. 148–149)

Practice in encoding, or translating sounds into letters (i.e., spelling), is directly related to better decoding, or changing letters into sounds (i.e., reading). In other words, writing (making sound-to-letter associations) and reading (making letter-to-sound associations) are clearly reciprocal processes.

As we know, phonological awareness precedes reading. When children learn to hear words and word parts and begin to understand the match between what they hear and what they see, the speech-print connection begins to make sense. When children construct words with alphabet blocks or tiles or with plastic letters, they are practicing phoneme-grapheme associations. In other words, they are giving a familiar word (something known) a label using abstract letters (something unknown). In the example of *dog*, the child says /dog/, thinks about a dog he or she knows (using schema), and attempts to spell the word *dog*. Initially, the child may write the word as *dg*, but as speech-print connections become automatic he or she will learn to write it correctly. Of course, the more experiences children have with this word-building process, the easier spelling and reading become. The opportunity to play with and manipulate letters and sounds is critical in beginning literacy. Activities involving objects, pictures, and the manual alphabet (sign language) strengthen sound-symbol associations (see Figure 5.2).

Color-highlighting vowels in red, digraphs in blue, and blends in green is also helpful. Highlighting or tracing vowels (*a, e, i, o, u,* and sometimes *y* and *w*), consonant digraphs (*sh, ch, th, wh*), and blends (*bl, cr, sk, str, nd, st,* etc.) in various colors can help children begin to recognize similar parts of words and understand their functions (see Figure 5.3).

When introducing vowels, it is important to include both long and short sounds—understanding that the letter *a* is sometimes long as in *ape* and sometimes short as in *apple* is a critical component to mastering the alphabetic principle. The earlier children grasp this aspect of language, the easier it will be for them to shift vowel sounds and decode accurately. (Note that *y* and *w* are included along with the common vowels because they function as vowels when occurring after another vowel or at the end of a word or syllable, as in *day, key, snow, boy, new, down, fly,* and *candy.* See the Vowel Patterns section for more about vowels.)

As children become comfortable with synthetic phonics, many games can be used with them to help them automatize sound-symbol connections. When children are able to construct the word *cat,* they can be taught new words by, for example, asking them to change *cat* to *bat.* Many rhyming words, such as *fat, hat,* and *rat,* can be spelled by changing only the initial letter. The same substitution activity can be used for final sounds: "If this is *cat,* can you show me *cab*?" Medial (vowel) sounds also can be practiced: "If this is *cab,* can you show me *cub*?" After the basic consonant-vowel-consonant (CVC) pattern has been mastered, initial blends can be introduced: "If this is *bag,* can you show me *flag*?" Many children enjoy this type of activity, especially when using plastic letters, letter chips, blocks, cards, or similar alphabet manipulatives. In all skill instruction, we strongly recommend using words with which the children are familiar and to which children have been exposed in a Big Book, story, poem, chant, or other print source. Moving from the known to the unknown and the familiar to the unfamiliar should be fundamental to introducing any new skill.

Analytic Phonics

Analytic phonics is the second component of the graphophonic triad. It is an instructional approach that introduces words initially as wholes and then separates the sounds and letters into familiar patterns. As students discover letter-sound relationships and patterns, they learn to manipulate these parts to form wholes. In other words, segmentation of

Vowels	Digraphs	Blends
a	sh	bl-
e	ch	cl-
i	th	fr-
o	wh	pr-
u	ph	spl-
-y		-nd
-w		(etc.)

Figure 5.3 Vowels, Digraphs, and Blends

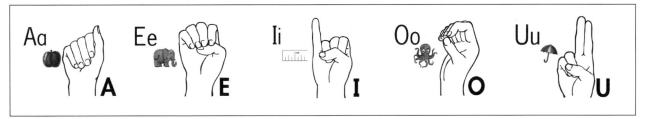

Figure 5.2 Manual Alphabet Representations of the Common Vowels

whole words and blending of word parts occur almost simultaneously. For example, when reading a story with several words from the same word family (rime or phonogram), such as *Dan, can, man,* and *ran,* a teacher might help children discover the *an* pattern. Previous phonological and print awareness provide a basis for analytic phonics instruction.

Analytic phonics programs include

- emphasis on whole-to-part-to-whole learning;
- dependence on phonological and print awareness;
- dependence on synthetic phonics knowledge;
- a combination of implicit and explicit phonics instruction;
- practice with decodable text; and
- awareness of spelling patterns.

Instruction in analytic phonics involves fostering an awareness of onsets and rimes and showing children how to "decode by analogy" (Cunningham 1995). By using a known phonogram (onset or rime), children are better able to decode unknown words. For example, if a child knows the word *beep,* she or he may decode the word *creep* by analogy, recognizing the rime *-eep* and substituting the onset *cr-* for *b-*. Many children think along these lines: "I know that says *jump,* so this must be *bump.*" The ability to recognize even as few as thirty-seven rimes (see Figure 5.4) helps children decode over 500 primary words (Wylie and Durrell 1970).

Vowel Patterns

The vowel pattern teaching approach is the third component of the graphophonic triad. This is the most sophisticated level of graphophonic analysis because it requires understanding syllable patterns and applying that understanding in the decoding process. A vowel pattern is a word or syllable that is decoded according to the position of its vowel(s) and consonant(s). Vowel patterns are also sometimes referred to as *spelling* or *syllable patterns.*

Although these syllable types are governed by a set of rules, it is their unique *pattern* that is recognized and applied in daily reading. May suggests that it is better for children to learn vowel patterns than rules because children "do not recite rules in their heads as they decode. They see clusters of letters that remind them of known words or known phonograms or known vowel patterns" (1998, p. 155). He continues, "Instead of rules, they need strategies for finding recognizable clusters of letters in words; teaching them vowel patterns provides them with a strategy" (p. 157). It is this strategy that empowers children to unlock the alphabetic code so that they can access the meaning of what they read.

Teaching vowel patterns has been very successful with many children, including those with reading disabilities. The approach is highly visual—children learn to recognize the *position* of the vowel(s) within words. Identifying vowel patterns enables readers to determine whether

Nearly 500 primary-grade words can be derived from the following set of only thirty-seven rimes (Adams 1990):

-ack	-ail	-ain	-ake	-ale	-ame	-an	-ank
-ap	-ash	-at	-ate	-aw	-ay	-eat	-ell
-est	-ice	-ick	-ide	-ight	-ill	-in	-ine
-ing	-ink	-ip	-it	-ock	-oke	-op	-ore
-ot	-uck	-ug	-ump	-unk			

Figure 5.4 Thirty-Seven Basic Rimes

a word is, for example, *met* or *meat*, *mad* or *made*, *got* or *goat*, and so forth. A strong point in favor of teaching vowel patterns is that once the concepts are learned and the patterns become automatic, thousands of words can be recognized, making it unnecessary to teach each and every rime or phonogram as a separate entity. An effective way to focus attention on vowel patterns is to highlight (or code) in red all vowels in words. This practice is temporary and should be discontinued when no longer necessary.

The vowel pattern chart shown in Figure 5.5 provides a structure, or scaffold, with which to classify the various vowel patterns. Once children realize that there are only six basic vowel patterns that can be analyzed and recognized fairly easily, the mystery of decoding disappears. A detailed description of each pattern follows.

Closed Vowel Pattern

Definition: a word or syllable that contains only one vowel and is followed by one or more consonants

Jingle: One lonely vowel squished in the middle says its special sound just a little.

Examples: *sat, bed, fin, top, gum, sand, best, print, shop, bunch, at, in*

The jingle above helps some children remember this pattern. A sandwich analogy provides another multisensory association that can help students learn this pattern. Using your hands as the bread and a child's hand as the filling, explain that a closed word (or syllable) is like a sandwich. A sandwich has two slices of bread and a filling in the middle. A closed word usually has a

consonant (show your left hand, palm up), a vowel (ask a child to place a hand on yours), and another consonant (place your right hand, palm down, on top of the child's hand and press firmly). The vowel is squished in there by this consonant (show your hand on top). Since it can't get out (it is closed in), it can only say its special (short) sound. Demonstrate with words from a familiar story and encourage student participation. In the words *cat, fast, lunch,* and *stop,* there is, in each word, only *one* vowel *and* it is followed by one or more consonants, so the vowel says its special sound, which is the short vowel sound. Short vowel sounds can be taught with associative picture clues, gestures, and sign language. For younger children, the term *short vowel* is not used, since they may confuse the concept with stature. *Special sound* is an easier concept for most children to understand and remember. Color highlighting provides another visual cue. To emphasize the position of a vowel within a word or syllable, highlight it in red.

Once children become familiar with the closed vowel pattern, they will be able to recognize many new words. Since most early literacy books contain many closed vowel pattern words, they offer numerous opportunities to reinforce this strategy daily.

Closed	Open		Silent *e*
Bossy *r*	**Two Vowels**		**Consonant + *le***
	Talkers (Vowel digraph)	**Whiners** (Vowel diphthong)	

Memory words:

Figure 5.5 Vowel Pattern Chart

Open Vowel Pattern

Definition: a word or syllable that ends with one long vowel
Jingle: If one vowel at the end is free, it pops way up and says its real name to me.
Examples: *me, she, hi, go, I, a, fly, sky, flu*

In this pattern, there is only one vowel at the end of the word, and no other letter follows it, so it is free to "pop up" and say its real name (its long vowel sound). The term *long vowel* may confuse younger children. Since long vowels "say" their own letter names, the term *real name* may be used instead. The word *me* has only *one* vowel *and* it's at the end, so it says its name. Other open vowel pattern words are *go, she, I,* and *sky.* The sandwich analogy can be applied again to this vowel pattern. If children are not familiar with the concept of an open sandwich, explain that it is a slice of bread with meat or cheese on top. It may have mustard or mayonnaise but it is *not* covered by another slice of bread. Explain that an open word or syllable is like an open sandwich. The bread on the bottom is the consonant (show your left hand, palm up), and the meat or cheese is the vowel (put the child's hand on top of yours). In this case, the vowel is free to "pop up" and say its real name (help the child raise his or her hand up in the air and say the vowel's name). Demonstrate with words from a familiar story, encouraging student participation.

As you introduce each new pattern, returning to the preceding pattern(s) is essential. This review provides the opportunity to discover similarities and differences among the various patterns. For example, most children quickly notice that both closed and open vowel pattern words have only one vowel, but in closed vowel pattern words the vowel has another letter (consonant) following it *(got/go, wet/we, him/hi)*. Reviewing learned patterns as you teach new ones also facilitates the realization that vowels can make more than one sound. The sooner children discover the different sounds of individual vowels, the easier it will be for them to unlock the alphabetic code and read with accuracy and fluency. Using words from familiar stories and practicing with alphabet manipulatives reinforces this concept.

Silent *e* Vowel Pattern

Definition: a word or syllable that has a vowel followed by a consonant followed by a final *e*
Story: The silent *e* is so powerful, it gives all its strength to the other vowel so that that vowel can say its real name. Since it gives away all its power, the final *e* is silent.
Examples: *make, Steve, ride, hope, cube*

In silent *e* words, the vowel before the *e* is long (it says its name). Use the story above to foster understanding and create an association that will help children remember this pattern. To demonstrate the relationship between the silent *e* pattern and the previously taught patterns, point out that the short vowel sounds in closed words become long vowel sounds (as in open words) with the addition of the silent *e* *(mad/made, kit/kite, hop/hope, cub/cube)*. Select examples of this pattern from familiar books to recall children's schema (what they already know) when you introduce a new and unfamiliar concept. Hands-on activities that encourage student involvement and participation bring the skill or strategy to life and increase learning. For example, you might ask children to come to the front of the room wearing letter cards and to make silent *e* words by arranging themselves in a row. The child with the silent *e* would use a "magic wand" to gently touch the child with the other vowel, allowing him or her to say its real name. Again, manipulatives reinforce a new skill and help children see the differences among the vowel patterns.

Double Vowel Talker Pattern

Definition: a word or syllable containing two adjacent vowels, the first of which is long
Jingle: When two vowels go walking, the first one does the talking—and says its name.
Examples: *rain, day, see, meat, pie, toe, slow, suit, blue, mail, green, boat, true, play, beat, doe, snow, fruit, lie*

Since children have learned the long vowel sounds (the vowels' "real names") in two of the previously taught patterns (open and silent *e*), this pattern follows easily because it, too, uses the long vowel sounds. Show children the visual pattern of two vowels next to each other and teach them the jingle: "When two vowels go walking, the first one does the talking—and says its name." Explain that the second vowel is quiet and just listens. In shared and guided reading text, have children identify this pattern and make word lists of additional examples of it. You might display these lists on a word wall for future practice and reference.

Double Vowel Whiner Pattern

Definition: a word or syllable that contains two adjacent vowels that do not say their long or short sounds but whine a very different sound

Story: Sometimes, when two vowels are next to each other, they make a funny whining sound, like when you fall down and say, "Ow," "Aw," "Oy," or "Boo-hoo."

Examples: *fault, saw, joy, foil, loud, down, cool, look, new, haul, paw, boy, coin, out, cow, moon, book, flew, launch, straw, toy, mouth, tooth, good, grew*

To reading specialists, double vowel whiners are known as *variant vowel digraphs* and *diphthongs*. Children easily make the association between the vowels and a whining sound.

Notice that the letter *w* works like a vowel when it follows a vowel, as in *paw* and *cow*. This is the reason for including *y* and *w* as "sometimes vowels" when teaching children the vowels. Children need much practice reading and manipulating these patterns. Again, using words from familiar stories and print around the room can make learning this and other patterns meaningful and somewhat easier. Remember that the goal is *not* to memorize rules but to recognize visual patterns so that decoding becomes accurate and fluent.

Bossy *r* Vowel Pattern

Definition: a word or syllable containing a vowel followed by *r* in which the vowel sound is altered by the *r*.

Story: The letter *r* is so bossy that it won't let the vowel say its short (special) or long (real name) sound, but must say a different sound, as in *car*.

Examples: *car, her, first, horn, curl, sharp, clerk, shirt, storm, churn*

The reason so many first attempts at spelling the word *car* (or any *r*-controlled

word) do not include a vowel is that children do not hear a short or long vowel sound in the word. Until children reach the visual spelling stage and have had many experiences seeing a particular *r*-controlled word, they may omit the vowel. The bossy *r* words are sometimes confused for closed words because they contain one vowel that is followed by another letter. Again, much practice with this pattern is necessary to insure automaticity. It is usually easier to begin with *-ar* and *-or* words and then include the "*-er* girls" (*-er*, *-ir*, *-ur*). The *-er* girls sound the same but look different. Of the three, *-er* is used most frequently, followed by *-ir* and *-ur*. Using familiar text and manipulatives fosters understanding of this pattern.

Consonant + *le* Vowel Pattern

Definition: a two-syllable word that ends with *le* preceded by a consonant

Story: When a word ends with a consonant and an *le*, the *le* grabs the consonant before it, and we break the word into two parts right before that consonant.

Examples: *ap-ple, bub-ble, ca-ble, ti-tle, ea-gle, pur-ple*

This syllable pattern occurs in many two-syllable words such as *tumble, bugle, turtle,* and *eagle*. (Before introducing this vowel pattern, you may need to review the concept of *syllable*.) To demonstrate this pattern, select a consonant + *le* (often shortened to C + *le*) word from a familiar story and write it on the board, drawing attention to its ending. For example, in the word *turtle*, the *le* grabs the consonant before it, breaking the word into two parts, or syllables: *tur-tle*. When the two syllables are blended, children hear the whole word *turtle*. Many words contain this pattern, and it is applicable to all words ending with a consonant followed by *le*.

Most children enjoy learning this pattern because it characterizes words that are longer and more sophisticated. You might have children cut a C + *le* word written on a word card into two parts. This provides a concrete, hands-on experience of the pattern that fosters an understanding of syllables. Group and individual charts can be created for future reference and review.

The ability of a young reader to pronounce new words based on an understanding of vowel patterns offers even more reason for including vowel pattern instruction in early reading programs. May (1998, p. 194) finds that "the prediction power of the five patterns ranges from 77 percent to 89 percent, each of which is much better than predictions on the basis of chance alone. Teaching children vowel patterns can make a difference in their fluency and comprehension."

It is interesting to note that thirty-five of the thirty-seven basic rimes (see Figure 5.4) conform to three common vowel patterns: closed, silent *e*, and double vowels (see Figure 5.6). Rather than teach each rime as a separate entity, you might simply teach these three patterns, which will enable children to recognize a vast number of unfamiliar words. Once children understand the *concept* of these patterns, they will easily recognize most words found in early literacy books. The fact that twenty-two of the thirty-seven basic rimes are closed patterns reveals the importance of short vowels. The only two basic rimes that do not conform to the vowel patterns are *-ight* and *-ore*, which can be taught as special patterns or irregular words, as discussed below.

Special Patterns

There are several special patterns that occur fairly frequently in reading and writing. They do not conform exactly to the common vowel patterns as described previously and may be taught as additional patterns. These special patterns include the following rimes: *-all, -alk, -igh, -ight, -ild, -ind, -old, -ost.* By collecting words from stories and brainstorming other words that fit these patterns, your children can make class charts or word walls that will assist them in recognizing these special patterns.

Irregular Words

A small percentage (about 15 percent) of words do not follow the five vowel patterns or the special patterns mentioned. In these words, it is usually the vowel part of the word that is truly irregular, as in *to, the, have, said, come, one,* and *was.* These words can be taught through context, repetition, and multisensory techniques (see Chapter 4). Since these words do not conform to the regular vowel patterns (and don't follow the rules), they are often called *memory words* or *unfair words.* When using the vowel pattern chart (see Figures 5.5 and 5.6) to classify words from a story, write these memory words below the chart. Some children enjoy circling the words to indicate their "noncompliance."

An effective way of teaching irregular words, as well as other unfamiliar words, is to encourage students to use all cueing systems simultaneously rather than rely heavily on one. Encourage students to ask, "Does the word make sense?" (semantic), "Does it sound right?" (syntactic), and "Does it look right?" (graphophonic).

Closed			Open		Silent *e*	
-ack	-ick	-ock			-ake	-ice
-an	-ill	-op			-ale	-ide
-ank	-in	-ot			-ame	-ine
-ap	-ing	-uck			-ate	-oke
-ash	-ink	-ug				
-at	-ip	-ump				
-ell	-it	-unk				
-est						

Bossy *r*	Two Vowels		Consonant + *le*
	Talkers (Vowel digraph)	**Whiners** (Vowel diphthong)	
	-ain	-aw	
	-ail		
	-ay		
	-eat		

Memory words: -ight
-ore

Figure 5.6 Vowel Pattern Chart of the Thirty-Seven Basic Rimes

Teaching Suggestions

You may find the following activities helpful in teaching graphophonic analysis in your classroom.

- Make an alphabet box and have students collect small objects that begin with each letter of the alphabet to put in it. Make a word card for each object and have students match words to objects.

- Select one-syllable words from a story and have students construct the words with magnetic letters or other alphabet manipulatives (if possible, use red for vowels).

- Write selected words from a story on sticky notes and have students match them to words in the text.

- Select words from a story and ask students to change them to new words, using letter tiles or chips.
  - Initial-consonant substitutions: change *sun* to *fun*
  - Final-consonant substitutions: change *sun* to *sub*
  - Medial-vowel substitutions: change *fun* to *fan*
  - Additions: change *bug* to *bugs*
  - Deletions: change *stop* to *top*

  To review phonemic manipulation, students can begin this activity with plain blocks or tiles to indicate sounds only and then add letter chips to show symbol-sound relationships.

- Select a rhyming word such as *stop* from a story and have students brainstorm words that rhyme with it. List rhyming words on a class chart, highlighting the rhyming parts in bright colors. Display the chart for future use.

- Select several closed vowel pattern words from a story, such as *hen, big, red,* and *hop.* Have students construct these closed words with alphabet chips (prepare chips with vowels in red so that the vowel pattern will be obvious). Have students make a "sandwich" with letter chips and observe the vowel being "squished" in the middle. Encourage students to repeat the activity with closed vowel pattern words they think of on their own.

- Make word cards of selected vowel pattern words from a story. Put magnetic tape on the backs and have students take turns placing them on a large vowel pattern chart on a magnetic board. Children can write the words on individual vowel pattern charts at their seats. As students classify words, have them verbalize the reasons for their choices.

- Give each student a letter card and ask students to arrange themselves in a row to spell various words from a story. Then change a part of the word and have students rearranged themselves appropriately (phonemic manipulations).

- Play variations of the hangman game. Draw the correct number of dashes on the board (red dashes for vowels) and have children guess the word. Each dash can represent an individual sound or letter (e.g., *boat* could be represented by three dashes for the three sounds or by four dashes for the four letters).

- Have students locate and frame specific pattern words in the Big Book using color highlight tape, a magnifying glass, a window card, or other manipulatives.

Chapter 6

Structural Analysis: Expand It

As children progress in their reading and writing abilities, they encounter new and more sophisticated print. The same patterns and strategies they use to decode one-syllable words can be transferred to more complex, multisyllabic words. For example, the compound word *fireman* contains the silent *e* word *fire* and the closed word *man*. The word *prepayment* contains the prefix *pre*, which is an open syllable; the root word *pay*, which is a double vowel talker; and the suffix *ment*, which is a closed syllable. When seen as two or three familiar chunks instead of as totally new and unfamiliar entities, multisyllabic words become easy to decode and understand. As children begin to analyze words, they discover that big words contain little words. Cunningham explains that "good readers…look for chunks based on words they already know" (1995, p. 122). Thus, when taught in a balanced model of instruction, decoding multisyllabic words becomes part of the whole learning process.

This chapter addresses structural analysis, which encompasses root words and affixes (prefixes and suffixes), compound words, contractions, and syllabication (see Figure 6.1).

Root Words and Affixes

Root word: the stem or the base word that remains after all prefixes and suffixes are removed (e.g., *un***friend***ly*)

Affix: a prefix or suffix

Prefix: one or more letters or sounds that are added to the beginning of a word and which change the meaning or grammatical function of the word (e.g., ***re****write*, ***pre****view*); common prefixes are *un*, *re*, *dis*, *mis*, *de*, *im*, *in*, *pre*, *sub*, and *trans*

Suffix: one or more letters or sounds that are added to the end of a word and which change the meaning or grammatical function of the word (e.g., *sleep***less**, *teach***er**); common suffixes are *s*, *ed*, *ing*, *ful*, *less*, *ly*, *ness*, *able*, *er*, and *or*

As children progress to more difficult levels of reading (decoding) and writing (encoding), their knowledge of multisyllabic words becomes more important. Understanding root words, prefixes, and suffixes helps children decode accurately and fluently and expands their reading and writing vocabulary.

To introduce the concept of root words, select an appropriate word, such as *unhappy*, from a familiar story. As students discuss the story and the character who is unhappy, ask them to find the part of the word they may already know *(happy)* and draw a green box around the prefix *un*. (Since the color green indicates *go*, it may help students remember that the prefix comes at the beginning of words.) Ask them the meaning of *unhappy* and help them discover that *unhappy* is the equivalent of *not happy*. Explain that a prefix is

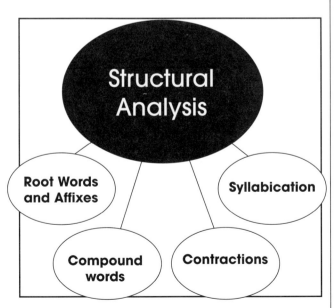

Figure 6.1 The Components of Structural Analysis

simply a letter or syllable that is added to the beginning of a main word, or root word, that changes the word's meaning (in this case, to its opposite). Have students list other *un* words in which the root word is changed to its opposite (e.g., *unkind, unhealthy, unfair*). When you encounter other words containing prefixes, have students add them to their lists. You may wish to create a class list containing prefixes and root words and add it to the word wall.

Similar activities can be carried out for suffixes. As children locate the suffix in a word, ask them to draw a red box around it. (Since the color red indicates *stop*, it may help students remember that the suffix comes at the end of words.) The technique of drawing a box around affixes can help children see the pattern in words. If children have difficulty decoding particular prefixes, suffixes, or root words, it may help to review and apply the vowel patterns (e.g., *reheat* is simply an open syllable and a double vowel talker). Activities with manipulatives and word games can provide needed review and reinforcement. A reproducible version of the structural analysis chart shown in Figure 6.2 is provided in Appendix 1 and can be used as a blackline master or classroom wall chart to classify various root words and affixes.

Compound Words

Compound word: a word that is composed of two words that can stand alone
Examples: *fireman, doghouse, backyard, milkshake, outside, blackboard*

One way to introduce syllabication is through compound words. Beginning with words the children already know from a familiar story or print experience, demonstrate how some big words are merely two little words put together.

Cut familiar compound words, such as *inside* and *backpack*, into little words, while saying each part. Then put them back together, saying the compound word. Have children locate other compound words in stories and list them on charts or on the word wall. You might use interconnecting puzzle pieces or blocks for a hands-on activity in which children practice the concept of putting together two little words to make one new big word. You may want to list familiar compound words in the structural analysis chart (Figure 6.2).

Contractions

Contraction: a single word formed by combining two words and deleting one or more letters, with an apostrophe in place of the deleted letter(s)
Examples: *can not = can't; I am = I'm; is not = isn't; he is = he's*

Children discover contractions early on in their reading experiences. Since contractions are used frequently in oral language, many children are able to make this speech-print connection implicitly. Other children, however, require more explicit instruction.

To demonstrate the concept of contractions, select a familiar contraction, such as *can't*, from a poem or story students know. Write it on the board, highlighting the apostrophe in red. Ask children to read the sentence that contains the word. Read along with them, emphasizing *can't*. Read it again, substituting *can not* for

Prefixes	Root words	Suffixes	Compound words	Contractions
un-	friend	-ly	milkshake	can't

Figure 6.2 Structural Analysis Chart

38

can't, allowing the children to discover that the meaning is not changed. Write *can not* with the second *n* and the *o* in red. Compare the two words, demonstrating that the apostrophe takes the place of the *no* in *not* and that *can't* is a short way to say *can not*. To make this concept more obvious, stretch a rubber band while saying the two words (long form), and let it go while saying the contraction (shortened form). Encourage children to locate other contractions in various stories. Discuss their meanings and create a list. You might suggest that students look for contractions with the words *not*, *will*, *is*, *are*, and *am*. Children's lists may be displayed on charts, on a word wall, or in a collage. Elbow macaroni may be used as apostrophes to make charts more tactile.

Syllabication Patterns

Syllabication: a strategy of dividing words into syllables

C + *le* (consonant + *le*): This pattern occurs in two-syllable words that end with a consonant followed by *le*. The *le* "grabs" the consonant before it, and that's where the word is broken. Examples: *bub-ble*, *puz-zle*, *ta-ble*, *cra-dle*, *gar-gle*, *pur-ple*.

VC/CV (vowel and consonant/consonant and vowel): When two consonants appear between two vowels, we break between the consonants. Examples: *kit-ten*, *pup-pet*, *bas-ket*, *den-tist*.

V/CV (vowel/consonant and vowel): In this pattern, there is only one consonant between the vowels and we break before the consonant. Examples: *be-gan*, *di-ver*, *fi-nal*, *mu-sic*, *pa-per*, *ro-bot*.

VC/V (vowel and consonant/vowel): In this version of the previous pattern, there is again only one consonant between the vowels, but this time we break after the consonant. Examples: *cab-in*, *drag-on*, *lem-on*, *mel-on*, *rob-in*, *wag-on*.

V/V (vowel/vowel): Occasionally, when words contain two vowels next to each other, we divide between the vowels. Examples: *li-on*, *di-et*, *cre-ate*, *po-et*, *du-et*.

Traditionally, syllabication rules were taught to assist children in breaking up unfamiliar words. In accordance with the concept that the brain is a pattern detector and not a rule memorizer, we suggest using syllable patterns (a more visual approach) instead of rules to divide unknown, multisyllabic words. This approach involves the vowel and syllable patterns explained in chapter 5.

The syllabication chart shown in Figure 6.3 (and provided as a reproducible in Appendix 1) provides a structure to help children understand and differentiate among the various syllabication patterns. Encourage children, when they encounter an unfamiliar long word, to look for one of the following patterns and divide the word into familiar chunks.

C + *le*	VC/CV	VCV	
		V/CV	VC/V

Figure 6.3 Syllabication Chart

The C + le Pattern

The C + *le* pattern is discussed in detail in chapter 5. It occurs in many two-syllable words that end with a consonant followed by *le*. The words *bubble, puzzle, table, cradle, gargle,* and *purple* contain this pattern. In these words, the *le* grabs the consonant before it, and that is where the word is broken *(puz-zle, cra-dle, pur-ple).* Since children are already familiar with closed, open, and bossy *r* syllables, they should easily recognize the *puz, cra,* and *pur* parts of these words. Explain that the consonant slides into the *le* to make a */zul/, /dul/,* or */pul/* sound. Since this pattern occurs frequently and always works, children have many opportunities for application and transfer. Activities to reinforce this skill include cutting words into syllable parts, making syllable puzzles, and creating lists or charts of C + *le* words from stories and print around the room. Another worthwhile activity is using the syllable chart to classify the various types of syllable patterns.

The VC/CV Pattern

This syllable pattern also occurs frequently in children's literature. Examples of words with this pattern are *kitten, puppet, basket, dentist, magnet,* and *plastic.* To demonstrate this pattern, we use the "spot and dot" syllabication strategy shown in Figure 6.4.

Write a VC/CV pattern (e.g., *basket*) from a familiar story on the board. Color code the vowels in red and put a dot above each one (spot and dot each vowel). Then connect the dots and ask the children how many letters (consonants) are between the vowels. If the response is two, break between those two letters *(bas-ket).* Since the children are familiar with closed words, they should recognize *bas* and *ket* easily. Masking or covering one part while reading the other may be helpful to some students. This pattern may be practiced with puzzles, word cards, charts, lists, and so on.

---

1. **Spot and dot the vowels.**

2. **Connect the dots.**

3. **Look at the number of consonants between the vowels.**

4. **If two, break between the consonants.**

5. **If one, break after the first vowel;**

   if it doesn't sound right, move over one letter.

Examples:	winter	win-ter	VC/CV
	hotel	ho-tel	V/CV
	lemon	lem-on	VC/V
	fantastic	fan-tas-tic	VC/CV; VC/CV
	computer	com-pu-ter	VC/CV; V/CV
	tonsillitis	ton-sil-li-tis	VC/CV; VC/CV; V/CV

Figure 6.4 "Spot and Dot" Syllabication Strategy

The V/CV and VC/V Patterns

In the V/CV and VC/V patterns, there is only one consonant between the vowels. To demonstrate the more frequently occurring V/CV pattern, select a word (e.g., *began, diver, final, music, paper, robot, tiger*) from a familiar story to write on the board. Write the vowels in red. Apply the "spot and dot" strategy, but in this case there is only one letter (consonant) between the vowels, so break before that consonant: *ti-ger.* Since *ti* and *ger* are open and bossy *r* syllables (concepts that should already be known to students), children will easily read the word as *tiger.* Practice with puzzles, cutting words apart and putting them back together. Locating other V/CV words in stories and print and creating lists and charts can help students apply and transfer this skill.

In the VC/V version of the pattern, there is again only one consonant between the vowels, but the word is broken after the consonant. Since this pattern occurs less frequently than the V/CV version, it should be introduced after the other is established. Words that follow this pattern include *cabin, dragon, lemon, melon, robin,* and *wagon.* If a word does not make sense using the V/CV pattern, move over one letter and try again. For example, if the word *lemon* is divided before the *m,* the word becomes *le-mon* (pronounced *lee-mon*). Since there is no such word, try the second option, *lem-on.* Children need practice applying these patterns to see what makes sense in context. Using semantic and syntactic cues provides additional help with these multisyllabic words.

The V/V Pattern

This pattern occurs infrequently and may cause some confusion for beginning readers. It should be introduced after students have become familiar with the other more common patterns. Words following the V/V pattern are divided between the vowels; examples are *po-et, ru-in, fu-el,* and *cre-ate..* As with the other patterns, children need to use semantic and syntactic cueing systems to determine the correct pronunciation of words that fit this pattern. In many cases, students will try the other more common patterns before applying this one. It is important that teachers and children alike realize that phonics is only a guide for correct pronunciation, since English is at times inconsistent.

Focusing on examples of words that contain a combination of syllabication patterns can help clarify the importance and practicality of learning such patterns. If we apply the "spot and dot" technique to the word *professor,* we break between the *o* and *f* (one consonant between the vowels) and between the *s* and *s* (two consonants between the vowels). In other words, *professor* can be divided into *pro-fes-sor* (open, closed, and bossy *r* syllables), which are three familiar chunks. Similarly, when "spot and dot" is applied to the word *tonsillitis,* the breaks occur between the *n* and *s* (two consonants between the vowels), between the *l* and *l* (two consonants between the vowels), and between the *l* and *t* (one consonant between the vowels). In this way, *tonsillitis* can be divided into *ton-sil-li-tis* (closed, closed, open, and closed syllables), which are four familiar chunks. Children may use a vowel pattern chart (see Figure 5.5) to classify each syllable within a multisyllabic word, as shown in Figure 6.5. (See Appendix 1 for a reproducible vowel pattern chart.) With practice, children can apply these patterns to many multisyllabic words, becoming more fluent and accurate readers.

In summary, children can learn to decode more complex, sophisticated words by applying some basic rules of structural analysis. Practice with compound words, root words and affixes, contractions, and syllabication patterns can foster independent reading by helping students find little words or known patterns within bigger words. Discovering these skills in the context of familiar stories makes learning meaningful. When learning is meaningful, children have a better chance of remembering and transferring skills and information. And when transfer occurs, the goal of learning is achieved.

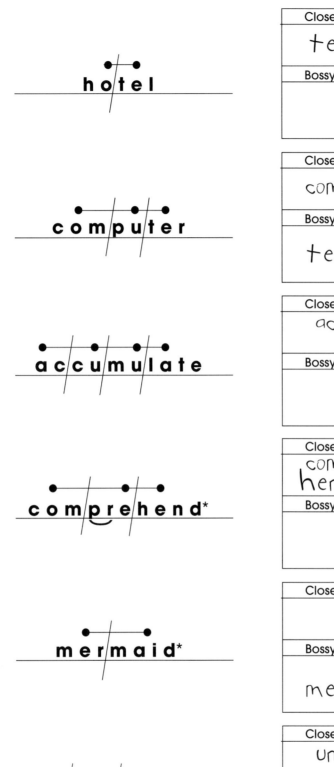

Closed	Open		Silent e
tel	ho		

Bossy r	Two Vowels		C + le
	Talkers	Whiners	

Closed	Open		Silent e
com	pu		

Bossy r	Two Vowels		C + le
	Talkers	Whiners	
ter			

Closed	Open		Silent e
ac	cu mu		late

Bossy r	Two Vowels		C + le
	Talkers	Whiners	

Closed	Open		Silent e
com hend	pre		

Bossy r	Two Vowels		C + le
	Talkers	Whiners	

Closed	Open		Silent e

Bossy r	Two Vowels		C + le
	Talkers	Whiners	
mer	maid		

Closed	Open		Silent e
un			

Bossy r	Two Vowels		C + le
	Talkers	Whiners	
der		stood	

*Blends, digraphs, and two vowels stay together.

Figure 6.5 Using Vowel Pattern Charts

42

Teaching Suggestions

You may wish to use the following activity suggestions to help teach students the patterns discussed in this chapter:

- From a familiar story, select a word that contains a root word and a prefix or suffix, such as *friendly*. Have students draw a box around the *ly* suffix and write the root word, *friend*, and the suffix in the appropriate sections of a structural analysis chart (see Figure 6.2 for a sample chart). Brainstorm and create a list of other *ly* words to include in the chart. Display the chart on the word wall.

- From a familiar poem or story, select several compound words, such as *something*, *everyone*, and *gateway*. Using two large, interconnecting puzzle pieces, write each little word on the puzzle pieces for children to fit together. Place children's puzzles on charts or mobiles for reference. Have students write the compound words in the structural analysis chart.

- Using multisyllabic words from a story, apply the "spot and dot" technique. Have students feel each syllable as they say it and write it in the appropriate section of the syllabication chart (see Figure 6.3) or the vowel pattern chart (see Figures 5.5 and 6.5).

- Using multisyllabic words from a story, make small puzzles from index cards. Have students cut big words into little chunks and reassemble the parts to recreate the original words. Have students read words and find them in the story.

- Using materials such as pipe cleaners, bendable wax strips, a magnifying glass, or window cards, have students frame specific words they find in a story.

- Have students use blocks to show the correct number of syllables in specific words from a story.

In *Reading Today*, the International Reading Association published its statement regarding the organization's views on phonics instruction (1997), which can be summarized as follows:

1. Teaching phonics is an important aspect of beginning reading instruction.

2. Classroom teachers in the primary grades do value and do teach phonics as part of their reading programs.

3. To be effective in promoting independence in reading, phonics instruction must be embedded in the context of a total reading and language arts program.

International Reading Association Vice President Kathryn Ransom adds, "The research continues to support the importance of phonics instruction for some young readers. The debate seems to be more related to the amount and form of instruction. The teacher must become a wise diagnostician and provide appropriate teaching and intervention for each child."

We strongly support and encourage systematic phonics instruction and sincerely hope that this book will provide teachers with the strategies they need to implement effective diagnostic teaching.

Part 2

Introduction

Assessment

Schools across the country spend considerable money, time, and effort administering, scoring, and interpreting tests. Many of these tests are developmental and are administered for purposes set by states and/or districts to determine achievement. These *norm-referenced* and *criteria-referenced tests* have been used for many years to find and compare strengths and areas of concern among large groups of learners. Traditionally, assessment has been associated with accountability and has not been integrated into daily instruction through *performance assessment.* However, recently there has been a great deal of effort to develop a set of assessment tools that are more closely related to daily instruction. This more individualized approach has created a demand for *curriculum-based assessment.*

What Assessment Experts Say

Assessment, according to Payne, concerns itself with the totality of the educational setting and subsumes the concepts of measurement and evaluation: "Assessment focuses not only on the nature of the learner, but also on what is to be learned and how" (1997, p. 5). Payne explains that measurement is concerned with systematic collection, quantification, and ordering of information. It implies both the process of quantification and the result. Measurement can take many forms, ranging from the application of very elaborate and complex electronic devices to paper-and-pencil exams to rating scales or checklists. Payne defines a *test* as "a particular form of measurement. Implicit in the term's current usage is the notion of a formal standardized procedure in which the examinee is aware that he is being tested for a particular purpose at a specified time. Normative data also tend to be presented along with the raw scores" (1997, p. 6). Evaluation is a general process for making judgments and decisions.

According to Payne, "a teacher can draw on classroom exams, anecdotal material, scores from standardized tests, and informal observations in arriving at a decision on the promotion of a pupil" (1997, p. 6). Payne calls educational assessment an "interpretive integration of application tasks (procedures) to collect objective-relevant information for educational decision making and communication about the impact of the teaching-learning process" (1997, p. 9).

Payne goes on to describe the general characteristics of modern assessment, which is often called *authentic assessment, direction assessment, alternative assessment,* or *performance assessment.* These characteristics include the following:

- Value beyond the assessment itself
- Student-constructed response
- Realistic focus
- Application of knowledge
- Multiple data sources
- Objective-based and criteria-referenced standards
- Reliability
- Multiple approaches
- Multidimensional structure
- Multidimensional scores

One method of modern assessment involves portfolios. Other assessment methods, thoroughly discussed in Hiebert and Taylor (1994), are interest surveys, observational checklists, interviews, conference forms, think-aloud protocols, literature logs, observation and analysis of records from projects, cooperative group activities, writing folders, and others too numerous to list. Hiebert and Taylor define *authentic assessment* as assessment activities that represent the literacy behavior of the community and workplace as well as the actual learning and instructional activities of the classroom. They define *performance assessment* as the demonstration by students of their level of competence or knowledge through the creation of a product or response (1994, p. 11). Their book is filled with excellent examples of the use of this assessment in various school programs as well as state-level programs in California, Arizona, and Maryland.

Choate wrote an excellent text on *curriculum-based assessment*, which she defines as "the process of determining students' instructional needs within a curriculum by directly assessing specific curriculum skills" (1995, p. 19) and as "the process of gathering information. For teachers, assessment is conducted for the purpose of deciding which skills to teach" (1995, p. 6). She recommends that this assessment include direct assessment of basic skills and be directly connected to programming or instruction. Choate gives the following reasons for using curriculum-based assessment (1995, p. 19):

1. It helps teachers determine what to teach.

2. It is efficient.

3. It facilitates evaluation of student progress, program effectiveness, and research.

4. It is both valid and reliable.

5. It increases student achievement.

6. It can be used to help make referral decisions.

7. It complies with the IDEA requirements for Exceptional Student Education.

Choate discusses the major principles of assessment and suggests that there are at least two important points to guide this aspect of the curriculum. One is to be sure that assessment is a positive experience for students and that both their strengths and weaknesses are identified. The second point is to not spend too much time on assessment. Choate believes that teachers should spend the majority of their time teaching, not testing (1995, p. 21), and that, to implement curriculum-based assessment in the classroom, teachers need to (1) know that curriculum; (2) establish the beginning point of assessment; (3) analyze the responses;

(4) select appropriate instructional strategies; and (5) schedule the instructional sessions and use effective teaching skills.

Choate's suggestions to teachers for implementing direct assessment are as follows (1995, p. 63):

1. Begin direct testing with the subject areas indicated by the teacher to be problematic.

2. Administer a survey test of specific tasks and analyze results to determine further testing.

3. Select the testing procedure that matches curriculum in both content and format.

In their Association for Supervision and Development (ASCD) publication on assessment, Marzano, Pickering, and McTighe (1993, p. 11) emphasize that assessment and learning are intimately tied: "The importance of changing assessment practices so they mirror the learning process becomes more clear when one realizes that students in American schools learn what they know they will be tested on." They continue by presenting a comprehensive discussion of assessment standards and by providing examples of performance tasks as well as numerous rubrics for assessment.

Torgeson (1998) presents a very thorough article in *American Educator* on the need for assessment of reading among young children and the need to allocate resources for early identification and prevention of reading problems. He discusses the fact that two general abilities are necessary for good reading comprehension: language comprehension and the ability to accurately and fluently identify words in print (1998, p. 32). Torgeson explains that poor readers have problems sounding out words and understanding and applying the alphabetic principle in deciphering unfamiliar words. He states that "good phonetic reading skills are necessary in the formation of accurate memory for the spelling patterns that are the basis of sight word recognition" (p. 33). Torgeson also points out that these common difficulties are frequently caused by weakness in processing the phonological features of language, and he recommends assessing children's phonological awareness, phonemic awareness, and phonemic segmenting and blending as well as letter knowledge. He suggests the following tests for assessment:

- *The Phonological Awareness Test* by Robertson and Salter (1995b)
- *The Test of Phonological Awareness* by Torgeson and Bryant (1994)
- *The Yopp-Singer Test of Phoneme Segmentation* (Yopp 1995)

In the same issue of *American Educator*, the action paper written by the Learning First Alliance Board of Directors strongly suggests that having every child reading is an attainable goal, pointing out that "early diagnostic assessments, beginning as soon as kindergarten, can be a useful tool to assure immediate intervention for the children who are identified as being at risk of reading failure" (1998, p. 55). The paper goes on to list the skills children need to develop in prekindergarten and kindergarten: language, background knowledge, appreciation of stories and books, concepts of print, phonemic awareness, and recognition of alphabet and letter sounds.

In discussing assessment, Valencia, Hiebert, and Afflerbach state that "one of the most prominent messages of the authentic assessment movement is that classroom-based assessment is powerful and important.... Situating assessment in the classroom, closest to instruction and to the learner, validates the notion that what students actually do in classrooms is a critical source of assessment information" (1994, p. 23).

The trend in early literacy education is toward more cohesive reading and language arts programs that are based on more contemporary concepts of assessment and instruction. While we believe there is still a need for schools and school districts to use standardized tests to determine academic progress across large populations of learners, we think that teachers are more interested in assessments that correlate more specifically with their instructional objectives. There are a variety of models and rubrics available that help teachers develop assessments. One model described by Pike, Compain, and Mumper (1997, p. 92) pro-

vides information using the following forms of data collection for instructional planning:

- Daily observations
- Anecdotal records
- Miscue analysis/running records
- Student self-evaluations
- Think-alouds
- Portfolios
- Conferences
- Information from parents
- Questionnaires, surveys, and inventories
- Teacher judgment
- Spelling analyses

Schools may not be in a position to replace more traditional norm-referenced standardized achievement tests with these kinds of informal, curriculum-based assessments, but for diagnostic and teaching purposes both forms of assessment are important. Often there are discrepancies between formal tests and the day-to-day progress teachers note during instruction. Tests and other forms of assessment are administered for different purposes and therefore do not and should not be expected to provide the same kind of information.

Part 2 Assessment Tools

The assessment and student profiles provided in Part 2 will enable teachers to accurately determine which of the many phonics subsets of skills have been learned as well as organize instruction with this information in mind. While the material in Part 2 represents only part of the curriculum-based assessment that can be used to monitor progress in reading, this type of assessment is crucial to the instructional process and necessary to prevent reading failure. Each child can be assessed in any or all areas of phonics, providing the teacher with a specific profile of instructional needs and a way to document progress. This assessment information can be a part of your portfolio of student progress and can readily be used by next year's teacher.

We provide directions for administration and scoring with each level. Upon completion of the testing, teachers should complete individual student profiles before planning instructional interventions. Each assessment item is coded to a lesson plan developed for the purpose of initiating skill instruction.

Instruction

The materials in this book represent a balanced, integrated model for teaching phonics skills directly and systematically. This model emphasizes instruction that focuses on good literature. Once children have enjoyed and internalized this literature, the teacher should initiate skill instruction. Some children need more explicit instruction and practice than others do. A variety of opportunities for skill application and transfer must be provided, and a whole-to-part-to-whole instructional format is strongly recommended.

Each of the four instructional levels in Part 2 includes an assessment of phonological awareness and print awareness and adds additional skill instruction components appropriate to that developmental level. While phonological awareness and print awareness skills instruction are developmentally most appropriate with beginning readers, some older children, in second through fifth grade, require remedial instruction in these areas. Children often advance to higher grades without sufficient phonological and print awareness for various reasons, including lack of maturational readiness, disruptive home circumstances, and inadequate instruction. It is important to remember that phonological and print awareness precede phonics instruction and provide the foundation upon which these higher associations are made.

The lessons in Levels 1 through 3 are designed for teachers to use with developmental readers from prekindergarten through second grade. The lessons in Level 4 are provided for use with struggling readers in grades three through five.

Developmental Level 1:
prekindergarten–kindergarten

Developmental Level 2:
kindergarten–first grade

Developmental Level 3:
first grade–second grade

Developmental Level 4:
third grade–fifth grade

At each level, lessons are coded to assessment items. Teachers can use these lessons as models for developing their own lessons suited to the particular needs of their students and using the reading materials already available in their schools. The teaching time for lessons will depend on students' skills and the amount of practice they require. It is important to remember that teaching a skill lesson is only a small part of the total instruction process. Teachers at the prekindergarten and kindergarten levels may spend several months on phonological awareness and print awareness activities. As the school year progresses, they may identify children who are ready for lessons in the higher levels and introduce those lessons as needed.

Ongoing assessment and related instruction should be provided according to the developmental level of individual children rather than according to a grade-level curriculum guide. Often teachers feel pressure to teach curriculum rather than to provide learning experiences for children. Our goal is to empower teachers to assess children's learning levels and provide instruction that is situationally appropriate. Therefore, while we include grade levels to provide some general guidelines, we urge teachers to move across levels as they identify individual children's instructional needs.

Teachers in the past successfully taught parts of the reading process, but this fragmenting often resulted in misunderstandings as well as misinstruction. Even experienced teachers often began phonics instruction with synthetic phonics. We now know that both phonological and print awareness instruction should precede synthetic phonics instruction. It is important for teachers to see phonics as a complex component of reading and be knowledgeable about all of its parts. Understanding of phonics appears to develop in young readers in a sequential way and, therefore, whole-class instruction may be too advanced for some students and too slow for others, depending on their developmental progress.

As students advance through the grades, teachers often assign more silent and independent reading. However, even older children benefit from teacher modeling and opportunities to verbalize their ideas. Comprehension is often greatly expanded by providing concept- and schema-related discussions before silent reading. Second- and third-graders, especially those with delays in auditory processing, need to hear stories read to them and be actively involved in their own learning by sharing their thoughts and feelings and through role-plays, chants, songs, and story retellings.

In grades two and three, instruction should include comprehension and vocabulary strategies in addition to continued explicit phonics instruction. The amount of new vocabulary presented in both literature and content-area materials becomes highly significant at this level. Specific instructional strategies should include activities that facilitate the embedding of words in children's long-term memories. Traditional vocabulary programs ask children to locate definitions in the dictionary, use the words in a sentence, and memorize them for a test on Friday. This process frequently does not result in long-term retention. Vocabulary activities that focus on children's prior knowledge as well as make connections to new knowledge will result in deeper understanding and better retention.

Level 1

Prekindergarten-Kindergarten

Teacher's Assessment

Sheets

Level 1 Developmental Assessment and Instructional Matrix

Assessment component	Subtests
Phonological awareness	**1.1 Rhyming Words** **1.2 Segmenting: Words in Sentences** **1.3 Segmenting: Compound Words** **1.4 Segmenting: Syllables** **1.6 Blending: Compound Words** **1.7 Blending: Syllables** **1.9 Phoneme Identification: Initial**
Print awareness	**1.1 Concepts of Print** **1.2 Letter Recognition: Uppercase** **1.3 Letter Recognition: Lowercase**
Synthetic phonics	**1.1 Consonants** **1.2 Long Vowels** **1.3 Short Vowels**
Analytic phonics	**1.1 Word Families: Matching**
Vowel patterns	**1.1 Closed**
Structural analysis	

Level 1 Student Profile

Phonological Awareness

Subtest	Pre-	Post-
1.1		
1.2		
1.3		
1.4		
1.6		
1.7		
1.9		

Synthetic Phonics

Subtest	Pre-	Post-
1.1		
1.2		
1.3		

Analytic Phonics

Subtest	Pre-	Post-
1.1		

Print Awareness

Subtest	Pre-	Post-
1.1		
1.2		
1.3		

Vowel Patterns

Subtest	Pre-	Post-
1.1		

Comments:

Name	Date
Grade	Teacher
Examiner	

Level 1 Informal Assessment of Phonological Awareness

Name

Date

Grade

Teacher

Examiner

Directions: Mark a + for a correct response and a – for an incorrect response. Each subtest has a practice item. The words the teacher says are in italics.

A passing score is 4 correct responses out of 6. If a student misses two or more items, instruction may be indicated. Correct responses are in parentheses.

Level 1 Informal Assessment of Phonological Awareness

1.1   Rhyming Words

Say "yes" if the words rhyme and "no" if they don't rhyme. Do these words rhyme? **pin, fin** (yes)

hat, pat (yes)	____	**sun, run** (yes)	____
man, can (yes)	____	**lamp, land** (no)	____
chair, floor (no)	____	**clock, block** (yes)	____

1.2   Segmenting: Words in Sentences

Clap your hands each time you hear a word: **Come to my house.** (4 claps)

I have a dog. (4 claps)   ____

The floor was wet and cold. (6 claps) ____

The cat ran up the hill. (6 claps)   ____

My house has a pool. (5 claps)   ____

Tigers are big and strong. (5 claps) ____

The baseball is round. (4 claps)   ____

1.3   Segmenting: Compound Words

I'm going to say a word that has two parts. Listen while I say it: **sunshine**. *Now tell me each part.* (sun - shine)

milkshake	____	**fireman**	____
railroad	____	**houseboat**	____
doghouse	____	**toothbrush**	____

Level 1 Informal Assessment of Phonological Awareness (continued)

1.4   Segmenting: Syllables

Listen while I say a word: **pencil.** *Now say the word and clap your hands for each part you hear.* (2 claps)

table (2 claps) _____   **picture** (2 claps) _____

chair (1 clap) _____   **bottle** (2 claps) _____

grass (1 clap) _____   **radio** (3 claps) _____

1.6   Blending: Compound Words

Listen while I say two words: **mail, box.** *Now say them together.*

cup, cake _____   **black, board** _____

some, thing _____   **blue, jay** _____

air, port _____   **space, man** _____

1.7   Blending: Syllables

Listen while I say two word parts: **bas - ket.** *Now say them together.*

ti - ger _____   **sta - tion** _____

cir - cus _____   **el - e - phant** _____

ea - gle _____   **ta - ble** _____

1.9   Phoneme Identification: Initial

Listen to the beginning sound in the word **soap.** *Say the beginning sound in the word* **soap.**

milk _____   **vacuum** _____

fish _____   **nest** _____

zoo _____   **suit** _____

55

Level 1 Informal Assessment of Phonological Awareness (continued)

Directions: Mark a + for a correct response and a – for an incorrect response.

Name	
Grade	Teacher
Examiner	Date

Level 1 Informal Assessment of Print Awareness (Concepts of Print Checklist)

Purpose

The purpose of the Concepts of Print Assessment is to help you evaluate students' understanding of the details of print as well as related behaviors. Emergent learners must completely grasp the concepts of print to experience success in reading. This checklist is designed to help familiarize you with these concepts so that you will know what to look for when observing students on a daily basis.

When to Use

Use the Concepts of Print Assessment as an ongoing observational tool at the beginning of the year and then quarterly to record and monitor students' growth in understanding print concepts.

How to Use

Prior to using this assessment, familiarize yourself with the types of tasks required on the checklist. Assess each child individually. Provide the student with a book that is somewhat familiar; using a familiar book is more meaningful to students.

   Read through the book, either together or with the student reading independently. During the reading, record your observations of the student's behaviors. Try writing with a different color each time you use the assessment to make the student's record easier to track.

   Several of the tasks on the Concepts of Print Assessment are also observable during shared reading, guided reading, and writing, and at other times throughout the day. As you observe a student demonstrating proficiency with a task, make a note of it to record later.

Scoring and Informing Instruction

A total of 23 items are assessed on the Concepts of Print Assessment. Score each item as follows:

+ = Understands concept (answers the question or performs the indicated behavior without hesitation)

√ = Needs review (answers the question or performs the indicated behavior with hesitation or with additional prompting)

− = Does not understand concept (cannot answer the question or perform the indicated behavior)

In addition, write down any comments that reflect the student's print behaviors.

Level 1 Print Awareness: Concepts of Print Checklist

Assess	Prompt the Student	Pre-	Post-	Comments
Book Concepts				
Cover of book	Show me how you hold a book.			
	Show me the front of the book.			
	Show me the name of the author/illustrator.			
	Show me the back of the book.			
Title	Show me the title.			
Title page	Show me the title page.			
Text Concepts				
Print tells a story	Where does the book tell the story?			
Concept of a word	Can you put your fingers around a word?			
	Can you find two words that are the same?			
	Where is the first word on this page?			
	Where is the last word on this page?			
Concept of letter	Can you put your fingers around a letter?			
	Can you tell me the names of some letters on this page?			

+ = Understands concept (answers the question or performs the indicated behavior without hesitation)

√ = Needs review (answers the question or performs the indicated behavior with hesitation or with additional prompting)

− = Does not understand concept (cannot answer the question or perform the indicated behavior)

Level 1 Print Awareness: Concepts of Print Checklist

Directions: Have the student read through a familiar book. During the reading, record your observations of the student's behaviors.

Name

Grade   Teacher

Examiner

Date

Level 1 Print Awareness:
Concepts of Print Checklist (continued)

Directions: Have the student read through a familiar book. During the reading, record your observations of the student's behaviors.

Name		Date
Grade	Teacher	
Examiner		

Level 1 Print Awareness: Concepts of Print Checklist (continued)

Assess	Prompt the Student	Pre-	Post-	Comments
Directionality				
Starting at beginning of book, finishing at end of book	Which page do we read first? Which page do we read last?			
Top to bottom of page	Show me where you start reading on this page.			
Left-to-right in sentence	Which way do we go when we're reading?			
Return sweep	Where do we go when we get to the end of the line?			
Left-to-right page sequence	Where do we go when we finish reading a page?			
One-to-one Correspondence	Read this sentence and point to each word as you read.			
	Did what you read match the number of words?			
Mechanics				
Capital letter	Can you find a capital letter?			
Lowercase letter	Can you find a small or lowercase letter?			
Period (.)	What is this mark called? What do you do when you see it?			
Comma (,)	What is this mark called? What do you do when you see it?			
Question mark (?)	What is this mark called? What does it mean?			
Exclamation mark (!)	What is this mark called? What does it mean?			
Quotation marks (" ")	What are these marks called? What do they mean?			
Score				

Level 1 Print Awareness: Letter Recognition Score Sheet

(use with Level 1 Print Awareness: Letter Recognition Student Sheet)

1.2 Uppercase   1.3 Lowercase

Letter	Pre-	Post-
M		
S		
F		
P		
A		
T		
K		
B		
G		
I		
N		
W		
D		
J		
O		
L		
C		
H		
U		
R		
V		
E		
Q		
Y		
X		
Z		
Score		

Letter	Pre-	Post-
m		
s		
f		
p		
a		
t		
k		
b		
g		
i		
n		
w		
d		
j		
o		
l		
c		
h		
u		
r		
v		
e		
q		
y		
x		
z		
Score		

Comments:

Confusions:

Unknown letters:

Level 1 Letter Recognition Score Sheet

Directions: Have the students point to each capital letter and name it. Repeat with the lowercase letters. Mark a + for a correct response and a – for an incorrect response. Add the + responses to determine the score.

Name _____ **Date** _____

Grade _____ **Teacher** _____

Examiner _____

Level 1 Informal Assessment of Synthetic Phonics

Directions: Mark a + for a correct response and a – for an incorrect response.

Name		Date
Grade	Teacher	
Examiner		

Level 1 Informal Assessment of Synthetic Phonics

(use with Level 1 Synthetic Phonics Student Sheet)

1.1 Consonants

Ask the student to point to each letter on the Student Sheet and tell you the sound each consonant makes. For the letters *g* and *c*, ask if the student knows another sound the letter makes.

Example: b (/b/)

	Pre-	Post-
m (/m/)		
s (/s/)		
t (/t/)		
d (/d/)		
n (/n/)		
f (/f/)		
p (/p/)		
j (/j/)		
h (/h/)		
g (/g/)		
g (/j/)		
b (/b/)		
w (/w/)		
l (/l/)		
r (/r/)		
c (/k/)		
c (/s/)		
k (/k/)		
v (/v/)		
y (/y/)		
q (/kw/)		
x (/ks/)		
z (/z/)		
Score		

1.2/1.3 Long and Short Vowels

Ask the student to look at each letter and tell you the sound it makes. Enter the response in the appropriate column, Long or Short. Then ask if the student knows another sound the letter makes.

	Pre-		Post-	
	Long	Short	Long	Short
a				
e				
i				
o				
u				
Score				

60

Level 1 Informal Assessment of Analytic Phonics

(use with Level 1 Analytic Phonics Student Sheet)

1.1 Word Families: Matching

Circle the word in the second column that is in the same word family as the words in the first column. **Fill, Jill, hill.** *Now which of the next three words is in that word family?* **pill, set, hop.** (pill)

Column 1	Column 2	
fat, mat, cat	**zip, met, sat** (sat)	_____
bit, sit, lit	**get, fit, hop** (fit)	_____
fight, light, might	**night, seats, parks** (night)	_____
hop, pop, top	**man, mop, mom** (mop)	_____
best, nest, vest	**tent, west, belt** (west)	_____

Level 1 Informal Assessment of Analytic Phonics

Directions: Mark a + for a correct response and a – for an incorrect response.

Name		Date
Grade	Teacher	
Examiner		

Level 1 Informal Assessment of Vowel Patterns

Directions: Ask the student to read each nonsense word. Mark a + for a correct response and a – for an incorrect response.

Name		Date
Grade	. Teacher	
Examiner		

Level 1 Informal Assessment of Vowel Patterns
(use with Level 1 Vowel Patterns Student Sheet)

1.1 Closed

I will show you some nonsense words. Read them to me.

fam	_____	ot	_____
het	_____	nust	_____
ish	_____	stim	_____

Level 1

Prekindergarten-Kindergarten

Student Assessment Sheets

Level 1 Print Awareness: Letter Recognition Student Sheet
1.2 Uppercase

M	S	F	P	A	T
K	B	G	I	N	W
D	J	O	L	C	H
U	R	V	E	Q	Y
X	Z				

1.3 Lowercase

m	s	f	p	a	t
k	b	g	i	n	w
d	j	o	l	c	h
u	r	v	e	q	y
x	z				

Level 1 Synthetic Phonics Student Sheet

1.1 Consonants

m	s	t	d	n
f	p	j	h	g
b	w	l	r	c
k	v	y	q	
x	z			

1.2/1.3 Long and Short Vowels

a	e	i	o	u

Level 1 Analytic Phonics Student Sheet

1.1 Word Families: Matching

Practice item:

fill	Jill	hill	pill	set	hop
fat	mat	cat	zip	met	sat
bit	sit	lit	get	fit	hop
fight	light	might	night	seats	parks
hop	pop	top	man	mop	mom
best	nest	vest	tent	west	belt

fam	**ot**
het	**nust**
ish	**stim**

Level 1

Prekindergarten-
Kindergarten

Lesson Plans

Level 1 Prototype Lessons

Level 1 Developmental Lessons

The lessons that follow are coded to the previous assessment items. Many different types of children's literature, such as those used for shared reading and guided reading, poems, songs, chants, and stories from home and/or the library are recommended for lessons. For simplicity, however, the following lesson plans are based on only two texts: *Jack and Jill* and *Little Boy Blue* (traditional rhymes available in the SUNSHINE™ series from The Wright Group).

These lesson plans are merely examples; teachers should develop their own lessons for whatever literature is planned for the week. Blackline masters are provided in Appendix 1 for use in developing lesson plans.

Level 1 Lesson Plan Format

Book title: *Jack and Jill*		
Process	Materials	Activity
Preread it		Do the picture walk. Discuss pictures.
Read it		Share the Big Book rhyme by reading it aloud.
Reread it		Ask children to join you when they are ready.
Discuss it		Ask the students, *What does **fetch** mean? What does **crown** mean? Why did they get a pail of water from the hill?*
React to it		Reproduce the book using the students' names. Innovate by having children fetch different things in the classroom. See if you can find words that rhyme with each name.
Code it	Following this lesson plan are skill lessons based on this book.	
Apply it		
Transfer it		

1.1 Rhyming Words

Coding lesson: phonological awareness
Skill: rhyming word identification
Title: *Jack and Jill*
Materials: Big Book or posters with rhymes and illustrations

Procedures:

1. After enjoying the book or poster and establishing comfort through the first five components of the Lesson Plan Format, ask the children to listen for the words that rhyme with *Jill (hill), down (crown), got (trot), bed (head)*.

2. Brainstorm other words that rhyme: *Jill, pill, still, fill, sill, mill, will; down, clown, gown; got, lot, pot, rot, hot; bed, Ted, led, said, fed, red.*

Transfer:

1. Look for rhymes in *Little Boy Blue.*

2. Find rhyming words: *horn, corn; sheep, asleep.*

3. Brainstorm other words that rhyme: *horn, born, mourn, torn; sheep, deep, creep, heap, reap.*

1.2 Segmenting Words in Sentences

Coding lesson: phonological awareness
Objective: segmenting of words in a sentence
Title: *Jack and Jill*
Materials: Big Book or poster

Procedures:

1. After repeated choral readings, ask children to listen as you clap the title: *Jack* (clap) *and* (clap) *Jill* (clap).

2. Repeat with children chanting and clapping for each word.

3. Continue line by line for the entire text.

4. If children clap twice for *water* (wa - ter), say the word as a whole and explain you are listening for whole words, but some words have more than one part. *Listen to **Jack**. How many parts? Listen to **water**. How many parts?*

5. Continue but stop to discuss when students clap for syllables instead of whole words.

Transfer:

Repeat the activity with *Little Boy Blue*. You can do this activity with any nursery rhyme or chant.

1.3/1.6 Segmenting and Blending Compound Words

Coding lesson: phonological awareness
Skill: segmenting and blending of compound words
Title: *Little Boy Blue* (because there are no compound words in *Jack and Jill, Little Boy Blue* is used)
Materials: Big Book or posters with rhymes and illustrations
Procedures: 1. After chanting the rhyme, ask students to listen while you read "under the haystack fast asleep." 2. Show a picture of a haystack. 3. Cut the picture into two parts, saying "hay stack." Put it back together, saying "haystack." 4. Ask students to say the word with you. 5. Explain that when two words come together to form a new word, we call it a *compound word.* Repeat the process with *sunshine, railroad,* and *blackboard.*
Transfer: Using *Jack, Be Nimble,* ask students to listen for the compound word *candlestick.* Repeat the activity with this word.

Coding lesson: phonological awareness

Objective: Segmenting and blending of syllables

Title: *Jack and Jill*

Materials: Big Book or poster

Procedures:

1. Ask children to listen carefully as you chant the rhyme.

2. Listen again for words that have one part: *Jack, and, Jill, went,* etc.

3. Ask children to put their hands under their chin. Have them feel how many times their chin moves when they say *up* (1), *the* (1), *of* (1), *water* (2).

4. Draw a picture of water on a strip and cut it in two parts. Say *wa - ter.* Then blend the two parts together.

5. Repeat with blocks, tiles, etc.

6. Repeat with other two-syllable words (*tumbling, after*).

7. Repeat with three-syllable words.

Transfer: Repeat with *Little Boy Blue,* using *meadow* (mea - dow), *after* (af - ter), *under* (un - der), and *asleep* (a - sleep).

Coding lesson: phonological awareness
Objective: identification of initial phoneme
Title: *Jack and Jill*
Materials: Big Book or poster with pictures

Procedures:

1. Choral read the rhyme.

2. Say the first line: "Jack and Jill went up the hill."

3. *Listen while I say two words that start with the same sound:* **Jack, Jill.** *Say them with me:* **Jack, Jill.** *Tell me another word that starts the same way.*

   As children give you a word, repeat it, and ask all the children to repeat it with you. Continue until you have five to six words.

4. Invite children to find or draw pictures of words that begin with the *j* sound (/dz/) and make a poster. Let children take turns pointing to all the words as they say them.

Transfer:

1. Repeat the activity with other pictures and initial sounds from this rhyme: *went, water, with; fetch, fell, fast; could, caper, covered.*

2. Using other rhymes, such as *Little Boy Blue,* repeat the activity with the picture poster: *boy, blue, blow; cows, come, corn* (add to *C* chart already started); *horn, haystack, he* (add to *H* chart already started).

Coding lesson: print awareness

Skill: concepts of print familiarity

Title: *Jack and Jill*

Materials: Big Book or poster; transparent plastic sheets; colored markers

Procedures:

1. During the skill segment of the lesson, ask students to

- show you where to start reading
- show you the direction (left to right) of reading
- show you a return sweep
- show you page sequence
- show you words and spaces
- show you top and bottom
- show you words and letters

2. Using Daily News, have children repeat the skill, covering the news with plastic and writing on it with colored markers.

Transfer: Repeat the activity daily with your Big Book shared reading lesson.

Coding lesson: print awareness

Skill: recognition of uppercase letters

Title: *Jack and Jill*

Materials: Big Book; wax-covered yarn; pieces of colored transparent tape; laminated word card with magnetic strip

Procedures:

1. After enjoying the story, have children come up one at a time to the book and find all the words with the uppercase letter *J.* Have the student put the wax-covered yarn around the word or cover it with a piece of transparent tape.

2. Go to the chart in the room on which you have the pictures of things that start with *J.* Using a laminated word card with a magnetic strip, write a *J* for each word. As students say the word, have them place the letter *J* by it.

3. Using your alphabet frieze with students' names, identify the letter *J* and read all the names that are there, using transparent tape to highlight the *J*s.

4. Give a student a pointer and have him or her point to all the *J*-words in the room.

Transfer:

1. Repeat the *J* activity with a new rhyme, story, or poem.

2. Repeat the activity with another uppercase letter from a new rhyme, story or poem.

Coding lesson: print awareness

Skill: recognition of lowercase letters

Title: *Jack and Jill*

Materials: transparency and overhead projector; wax-covered yarn or colored transparent tape; colored chalk

Procedures:

1. Highlight a lowercase letter such as the *a* in *Jack* on a transparency.

2. Ask a student to find that letter in another word (visual tracking) and either circle it with a piece of wax-covered yarn or cover it with colored transparent tape.

3. Have students repeat the activity on pieces of paper and then transfer them to the transparency.

4. Turn the overhead to the chalkboard. Students can use colored chalk on the board to circle the letters. This can be a center activity.

5. Add the lowercase letter to the alphabet frieze already up in the room; make a ribbon of words in the room that have that letter. Then color code the letter.

Transfer:

1. Repeat the activity with different letters.

2. Repeat the activity with Daily News.

3. Make the letter in clay, in shaving cream, on a sand tray, in glue, or on a screen.

1.1 Consonants

Coding lesson: synthetic phonics
Skill: consonant: sound-symbol association
Title: *Jack and Jill*
Materials: Big Book or posters with rhymes and illustrations

Procedures:

1. After enjoying the book or poster and establishing comfort through the first five components of the Lesson Plan Format, ask the children to find all the words that begin with /w/ such as *went, water,* and *with.*

2. List the words on the board or use pictures. Trace the first letter with green. Have students repeat the word after you say it, listening for the first sound. Let them form the letter in the air as they say each word.

3. Repeat with the following beginning consonants:

c /k/: could, caper, covered

b /b/: broke, brown

h /h/: home, head, he, his

f /f/: fetch, fell, fast

Transfer: Using other rhymes, such as *Little Boy Blue,* repeat the activity for the following consonants

b: boy, blue, blow

c: cows, corn, come

1.2 Long Vowels

Coding lesson: synthetic phonics
Skill: long vowels: sound-symbol association
Title: *Jack and Jill*
Materials: Big Book or posters with rhymes and illustrations; copies of *Jack and Jill* text; alphabet cards

Procedures:

1. In the nursery rhyme *Jack and Jill,* find the words that have long vowels: *pail, home, paper, broke, came, caper.*

2. Ask students to find the words on copies of *Jack and Jill* and to trace over each vowel in red. Have them say the word aloud as they listen for the vowel. Ask them to identify the vowel by holding up the alphabet card that has the vowel on it.

3. Make a list of other words with the same vowel: *came, tame, lame, fame, same; home, dome, foam; pail, fail, mail, tail, sail.*

4. Have students find other long vowels around the room.

Transfer: With the rhyme *Little Boy Blue,* repeat the activity for the following words with long vowels: *blow, sheep, hay, asleep.*

Coding lesson: synthetic phonics

Skill: short vowels: sound-symbol association

Title: *Jack and Jill*

Materials: Big Book or posters with rhymes and illustrations; alphabet cards

Procedures:

1. In the nursery rhyme *Jack and Jill,* find the words that have short vowel sounds: *Jack, Jill, up, hill, fetch, tumbling, after, got, did, trot, as, fast, went, his, with.*

2. Ask students to say each short-vowel word while listening for vowel sounds. Have students hold up the vowel card that matches the vowel in the word. Have students say the short vowel sound by itself and then listen for it in each word: *i—hill, Jill, did, with, his; o—got, trot; a—Jack, after, as, fast.*

3. Make a list of other short-vowel words that rhyme with the one practiced.

Transfer: With the rhyme *Little Boy Blue,* repeat the activity for the following short-vowel words: *little, in, meadow, is, after, under, stack, fast.*

1.1 Word Families: Matching

Coding lesson: analytic phonics
Skill: matching word families
Title: *Jack and Jill*
Materials: transparency and overhead projectors; charts of words that rhyme with *ill* and *crown.*

Procedures:

1. Show a transparency of the word *Jill.* Say the word and box in the *ill* part of it. Repeat with *hill.*

2. Using colored transparent tape, code the *ill* in all the words on the *ill* word chart.

3. Repeat with -*ot* (got, trot) and -*own* (down, crown, brown).

Transfer:

1. Using *Little Boy Blue,* repeat the activity with -*orn* (horn, corn) and -*eep* (sheep, asleep).

2. Using *Down by the Bay,* repeat the activity with -*ee* (bee, knee) and -*oose* (moose, goose).

1.1 Closed Vowel Pattern

Coding lesson: vowel patterns
Skill: recognition of the CVC closed vowel pattern
Title: *Jack and Jill*
Materials: Big Book or poster; copy of script on transparency and on paper for each student; red markers; vowel pattern chart on magnetic board; rainbow alphabet (color-coded paper clips)

Procedures:

1. On the script on the transparency and on students' copies, model finding CVC (Consonant-Vowel-Consonant) words, such as *Jill, hill, fell, got, bed, went, with, his,* and *did.*

2. Have students code the vowel in red as they repeat the closed vowel pattern jingle (see p. 31 in Part 1).

3. Give a word card to a student to place on the magnetic wall chart.

4. Repeat with each of the words from the text.

5. Make each word with the rainbow alphabet.

Transfer: Repeat the activity with other charts, books, songs, and wall products.

Level 2

Kindergarten-First Grade

Teacher's Assessment Sheets

Level 2 Developmental Assessment and Instructional Matrix

Assessment Component	Subtests
Phonological Awareness	2.1 Rhyming Words
	2.2 Segmenting: Words in Sentences
	2.3 Segmenting: Compound Words
	2.4 Segmenting: Syllables
	2.5 Segmenting: Phonemes
	2.6 Blending: Compound Words
	2.7 Blending: Syllables
	2.8 Blending: Phonemes
	2.9 Phoneme Identification: Initial
	2.10 Phoneme Identification: Final
	2.11 Phoneme Identification: Medial
	2.12 Manipulation: Deletion
Print Awareness	2.1 Concepts of Print
	2.2 Letter Recognition: Uppercase
	2.3 Letter Recognition: Lowercase

Synthetic Phonics	**2.1 Consonants**
	2.2 Long Vowels
	2.3 Short Vowels
	2.4 Consonant Digraphs
	2.5 Consonant Blends
	2.6 *R*-controlled Vowels
	2.7 Vowel Digraphs
	2.8 Diphthongs
	2.9 Phoneme Segmenting and Blending
Analytic Phonics	**2.1 Word Families: Matching**
	2.2 Word Families: Production
	2.3 Word Families: Substitution of Initial Letter
	2.4 Word Families: Substitution of Final Letter
	2.5 Word Families: Substitution of Medial Letter
Vowel Patterns	**2.1 Closed**
	2.2 Open
	2.3 Silent *e*
	2.4 Bossy *r*
	2.5 Double Vowel Talkers
	2.6 Double Vowel Whiners

Name	Date
Grade	Teacher
Examiner	

Level 2 Student Profile

Phonological Awareness

Subtest	Pre-	Post-
2.1		
2.2		
2.3		
2.4		
2.5		
2.6		
2.7		
2.8		
2.9		
2.10		
2.11		
2.12		

Print Awareness

Subtest	Pre-	Post-
2.1		
2.2		
2.3		

Synthetic Phonics

Subtest	Pre-	Post-
2.1		
2.2		
2.3		
2.4		
2.5		
2.6		
2.7		
2.8		
2.9		

Analytic Phonics

Subtest	Pre-	Post-
2.1		
2.2		
2.3		
2.4		
2.5		

Vowel Patterns

Subtest	Pre-	Post-
2.1		
2.2		
2.3		
2.4		
2.5		
2.6		

Comments:

Directions: Mark a + for a correct response and a – for an incorrect response. Each subtest has a practice item. The words the teacher says are in italics. A passing score is 4 correct responses out of 6. If a student misses two or more items, instruction may be indicated. Correct responses are in parentheses.

Name		Date
Grade	Teacher	
Examiner		

Level 2 Informal Assessment of Phonological Awareness

2.1   Rhyming Words

Say "yes" if the words rhyme and "no" if they don't rhyme. Do these words rhyme? **pin, fin** (yes)

hat, pat (yes)	_____	**sun, run** (yes)	_____
man, can (yes)	_____	**lamp, land** (no)	_____
chair, floor (no)	_____	**clock, block** (yes)	_____

2.2   Segmenting: Words in Sentences

Clap your hands each time you hear a word: **Come to my house.**
(4 claps)

I have a dog. (4 claps)   _____

The floor was wet and cold. (6 claps)   _____

The cat ran up the hill. (6 claps)   _____

My house has a pool. (5 claps)   _____

Tigers are big and strong. (5 claps)   _____

The baseball is round. (4 claps)   _____

2.3   Segmenting: Compound Words

I'm going to say a word that has two parts. Listen while I say it: **sunshine.**
Now tell me each part. (sun - shine)

milkshake	_____	**fireman**	_____
railroad	_____	**houseboat**	_____
doghouse	_____	**toothbrush**	_____

Date

Name

Grade   Teacher

Examiner

Level 2 Informal Assessment of
Phonological Awareness (continued)

Directions: Mark a + for a correct response and a – for an incorrect response.

Level 2 Informal Assessment of Phonological Awareness (continued)

2.4 Segmenting: Syllables

Listen while I say a word: **pencil***. Now say the word and clap your hands for each part you hear.* (2 claps)

table (2 claps) _____		**picture** (2 claps) _____	
chair (1 clap) _____		**bottle** (2 claps) _____	
grass (1 clap) _____		**radio** (3 claps) _____	

2.5 Segmenting: Phonemes

I will say a word: **mat***. Tell me each sound you hear in* **mat.**
Say /m/ - /a/ - /t/ with the student.

see (s - ee) _____		**ship** (sh - i - p) _____	
do (d - oo) _____		**side** (s - i - d) _____	
fat (f - a - t) _____		**city** (s - i - t - ee) _____	

2.6 Blending: Compound Words

Listen while I say two words: **mail, box***. Now say them together.*

cup, cake _____		**black, board** _____	
some, thing _____		**blue, jay** _____	
air, port _____		**space, man** _____	

2.7 Blending: Syllables

Listen while I say two word parts: **bas - ket***. Now say them together.*

ti - ger _____		**sta - tion** _____	
cir - cus _____		**el - e - phant** _____	
ea - gle _____		**ta - ble** _____	

92

Level 2 Informal Assessment of Phonological Awareness (continued)

2.8 Blending: Phonemes

Listen while I say some sounds: /a/ - /t/. Now say them together.

m - e	_____	**s - ea - t**	_____
s - o	_____	**d - o - g**	_____
f - i - sh	_____	**l - u - n - ch**	_____

2.9 Phoneme Identification: Initial

*Listen to the beginning sound in the word **soap**. Say the beginning sound in the word **soap**.*

milk	_____	**vacuum**	_____
fish	_____	**nest**	_____
zoo	_____	**suit**	_____

2.10 Phoneme Identification: Final

*Listen to the ending sound in the word **bus**. Tell me the ending sound.*

top	_____	**duck**	_____
pit	_____	**come**	_____
mug	_____	**house**	_____

Level 2 Informal Assessment of Phonological Awareness (continued)

Directions: Mark a + for a correct response and a – for an incorrect response.

Name		Date
Grade	Teacher	
Examiner		

Level 2 Informal Assessment of
Phonological Awareness (continued)

Directions: Mark a + for a correct response and a – for an incorrect response.

Date

Name

Grade   Teacher

Examiner

Level 2 Informal Assessment of Phonological Awareness (continued)

2.11 Phoneme Identification: Medial

*Listen to the middle sound in the word **meet**. Tell me the middle sound.*

cake	_____	**pat**	_____
boat	_____	**him**	_____
ride	_____	**set**	_____

2.12 Manipulation: Deletion

*Say the word **football**. Say it again but don't say **foot**. Say* ball *with the student.*

Say the word **houseboat**. Say it again but don't say **house**. (boat) _____

Say the word **tiger**. Say it again but don't say **ti**. (ger) _____

Say the word **coat**. Say it again but don't say **c**. (oat) _____

Say the word **billboard**. Say it again but don't say **board**. (bill) _____

Say the word **table**. Say it again but don't say **ble**. (ta) _____

Say the word **soup**. Say it again but don't say **p**. (sou) _____

Level 2 Print Awareness Informal Assessment (Concepts of Print Checklist)

Purpose

The purpose of the Concepts of Print Assessment is to help you evaluate students' understanding of the details of print as well as related behaviors. Emergent learners must completely grasp the concepts of print to experience success in reading. This checklist is designed to help familiarize you with these concepts so that you will know what to look for when observing students on a daily basis.

When to Use

Use the Concepts of Print Assessment as an ongoing observational tool at the beginning of the year and then quarterly to record and monitor students' growth in understanding print concepts.

How to Use

Prior to using this assessment, familiarize yourself with the types of tasks required on the checklist. Assess each child individually. Provide the student with a book that is somewhat familiar; using a familiar book is more meaningful to students.

Read through the book, either together or with the student reading independently. During the reading, record your observations of the student's behaviors. Try writing with a different color each time you use the assessment to make the student's record easier to track.

Several of the tasks on the Concepts of Print Assessment are also observable during shared reading, guided reading, and writing, and at other times throughout the day. As you observe a student demonstrating proficiency with a task, make a note of it to record later.

Scoring and Informing Instruction

A total of 23 items are assessed on the Concepts of Print Assessment. Score each item as follows:

+ = Understands concept (answers the question or performs the indicated behavior without hesitation)

√ = Needs review (answers the question or performs the indicated behavior with hesitation or with additional prompting)

− = Does not understand concept (cannot answer the question or perform the indicated behavior)

In addition, write down any comments that reflect the student's print behaviors.

Level 2 Print Awareness: Concepts of Print Checklist

Name

Date

Grade

Teacher

Examiner

Directions: Have the students read through a familiar book. During the reading, record your observations of the student's behaviors.

Level 2 Print Awareness: Concepts of Print Checklist

Assess	Prompt the Student	Pre-	Post-	Comments
Book Concepts				
Cover of book	Show me how you hold a book.			
	Show me the front of the book.			
	Show me the name of the author/illustrator.			
	Show me the back of the book.			
Title	Show me the title.			
Title page	Show me the title page.			
Text Concepts				
Print tells a story	Where does the book tell the story?			
Concept of a word	Can you put your fingers around a word?			
	Can you find two words that are the same?			
	Where is the first word on this page?			
	Where is the last word on this page?			
Concept of letter	Can you put your fingers around a letter?			
	Can you tell me the names of some letters on this page?			

+ = Understands concept (answers the question or performs the indicated behavior without hesitation)

√ = Needs review (answers the question or performs the indicated behavior with hesitation or with additional prompting)

− = Does not understand concept (cannot answer the question or perform the indicated behavior)

Level 2 Print Awareness: Concepts of Print Checklist (continued)

Assess	Prompt the Student	Pre-	Post-	Comments
Directionality				
Starting at beginning of book, finishing at end of book	Which page do we read first? Which page do we read last?			
Top to bottom of page	Show me where you start reading on this page.			
Left-to-right in sentence	Which way do we go when we're reading?			
Return sweep	Where do we go when we get to the end of the line?			
Left-to-right page sequence	Where do we go when we finish reading a page?			
One-to-one Correspondence	Read this sentence and point to each word as you read.			
	Did what you read match the number of words?			
Mechanics				
Capital letter	Can you find a capital letter?			
Lowercase letter	Can you find a small or lowercase letter?			
Period (.)	What is this mark called? What do you do when you see it?			
Comma (,)	What is this mark called? What do you do when you see it?			
Question mark (?)	What is this mark called? What does it mean?			
Exclamation mark (!)	What is this mark called? What does it mean?			
Quotation marks (" ")	What are these marks called? What do they mean?			
Score				

Level 2 Print Awareness: Concepts of Print Checklist (continued)

Directions: Have the student read through a familiar book. During the reading, record your observations of the student's behaviors.

Name _____ Date _____

Grade _____ Teacher _____

Examiner _____

Directions: Directions: Have the student point to each capital letter and name it. Repeat with the lowercase letters. Mark a + for a correct response and a – for an incorrect response.

Name		Date
Grade	Teacher	
Examiner		

Level 2 Print Awareness: Letter Recognition Score Sheet
(use with Level 2 Print Awareness: Letter Recognition Student Sheet)

2.2 Uppercase

Letter	Pre-	Post-
M		
S		
F		
P		
A		
T		
K		
B		
G		
I		
N		
W		
D		
J		
O		
L		
C		
H		
U		
R		
V		
E		
Q		
Y		
X		
Z		
Score		

2.3 Lowercase

Letter	Pre-	Post-
m		
s		
f		
p		
a		
t		
k		
b		
g		
i		
n		
w		
d		
j		
o		
l		
c		
h		
u		
r		
v		
e		
q		
y		
x		
z		
Score		

Comments:

Confusions:

Unknown letters:

Level 2 Informal Assessment of Synthetic Phonics

(use with Level 2 Synthetic Phonics Student Sheets)

2.1 Consonants

Ask the student to point to each letter on the Student Sheet and tell you the sound each consonant makes. For the letters *g* and *c*, ask if the student knows another sound the letter makes.

Example: b (/*b*/)

	Pre-	Post-
m (/*m*/)		
s (/*s*/)		
t (/*t*/)		
d (/*d*/)		
n (/*n*/)		
f (/*f*/)		
p (/*p*/)		
j (/*j*/)		
h (/*h*/)		
g (/*g*/)		
g (/*j*/)		
b (/*b*/)		
w (/*w*/)		
l (/*ll*/)		
r (/*r*/)		
c (/*k*/)		
c (/*s*/)		
k (/*k*/)		
v (/*v*/)		
y (/*y*/)		
q (/*kw*/)		
x (/*ks*/)		
z (/*z*/)		
Score		

2.2/2.3 Long and Short Vowels

Ask the student to look at each letter and tell you the sound it makes. Enter the response in the appropriate column, Long or Short. Then ask if the student knows another sound the letter makes.

	Pre-		Post-	
	Long	Short	Long	Short
a				
e				
i				
o				
u				
Score				

Level 2 Informal Assessment of Synthetic Phonics

Directions: Mark a + for a correct response and a – for an incorrect response.

Name	Date
Grade	Teacher
Examiner	

Level 2 Informal Assessment of Synthetic Phonics (continued)

Name | Date
Grade | Teacher
Examiner

Directions: Mark a + for a correct response and a – for an incorrect response.

Level 2 Informal Assessment of Synthetic Phonics (continued)

(use with Level 2 Synthetic Phonics Student Sheets)

Look at these letters. Tell me what sounds they make.
Example: st

2.4 Consonant Digraphs
2.5 Consonant Blends

	Pre-	Post-
sh		
ch		
th		
wh		
ph		
cl		
gr		
st		
bl		
sk		
Score		

2.6 *R*-Controlled Vowels

	Pre-	Post-
ar (/ar/)		
er (/er/)		
ir (/er/)		
or (/or/)		
ur (/er/)		
Score		

2.7 Vowel Digraphs

	Pre-	Post-
ai (/ā/)		
ee (/ē/)		
oa (/ō/)		
oe (/ō/)		
ie (/ē/)		
Score		

2.8 Diphthongs

	Pre-	Post-
oy (/oy/)		
ow (/ow/)		
oi (/oi/)		
ou (/ou/)		
Score		

2.9 Phoneme Segmenting and Blending

Sound it out. Now say the whole word.

	Pre-	Post-
m - e (me)		
g - o (go)		
s - a - t (sat)		
f - i - l (fill)		
m - e - n (men)		
n - e - s - t (nest)		
Score		

Level 2 Informal Assessment of Analytic Phonics
(use with Level 2 Analytic Phonics Student Sheets)

2.1 Word Families: Matching

Circle the word in the second column that is in the same word family as the words in the first column. **Fill, Jill, hill.** *Now which of the next three words is in that word family?* **pill, set, hop.** (pill)

Column 1	Column 2	Pre-	Post-
fat, mat, cat	zip, met, (sat)		
bit, sit, lit	get, (fit) hop		
fight, light, might	(night) seats, parks		
hop, pop, top	man, (mop) mom		
best, nest, vest	tent, (west) belt		
Score			

2.2 Word Families: Production

Write another word in the same word family as **hop** *and* **top**. (pop)
Add to these word families.

	Pre-	Post-
tip, lip		
make, bake		
sack, pack		
bell, tell		
dot, hot		
bump, jump		
Score		

101

Name		Date
Grade	Teacher	
Examiner		

Level 2 Informal Assessment of Analytic Phonics (continued)

Name | Date

Grade | Teacher

Examiner

Directions: Mark a + for a correct response and a – for an incorrect response.

Level 2 Informal Assessment of Analytic Phonics (continued)
(use with Level 2 Analytic Phonics Student Sheets)

2.3 Word Families: Substitution of Initial Letter

Show the student the word **sit.** *Look at the word* **sit.** *Change the first letter* **s** *to* **b.** *Say the new word* (bit) *and write it on the line.*

			Pre-	Post-
top	Change *t* to *m*	(mop)		
lip	Change *l* to *s*	(sip)		
car	Change *c* to *f*	(far)		
boat	Change *b* to *g*	(goat)		
meet	Change *m* to *b*	(beet)		
look	Change *l* to *b*	(book)		
joy	Change *j* to *t*	(toy)		
Score				

2.4 Word Families: Substitution of Final Letter

Show the student the word **sit**. *Look at the word* **sit**. *Change the last letter to* **p**. *Say the new word* (sip) *and write it on the line.*

			Pre-	Post-
lot	Change *t* to *g*	(got)		
pen	Change *n* to *t*	(pet)		
hip	Change *p* to *d*	(hid)		
shot	Change *t* to *p*	(shop)		
plug	Change *g* to *s*	(plus)		
meet	Change *t* to *k*	(meek)		
Score				

102

Level 2 Informal Assessment of Analytic Phonics (continued)

(use with Level 2 Analytic Phonics Student Sheets)

2.5 Word Families: Substitution of Medial Letter

Show the student the word **sit**. *Look at the word **sit**.*
*Change the middle letter to **a**. Say the new word* (sat) *and*
write it on the line.

			Pre-	Post-
make	Change *a* to *i*	(mike)		
ride	Change *i* to *o*	(rode)		
wade	Change *a* to *i*	(wide)		
mud	Change *u* to *a*	(mad)		
ten	Change *e* to *i*	(tin)		
stop	Change *o* to *e*	(step)		
Score				

Directions: Mark a + for a correct response and a – for an incorrect response.

Name		Date
Grade	Teacher	
Examiner		

Level 2 Informal Assessment of Vowel Patterns

Directions: Mark a + for a correct response and a – for an incorrect response.

Name

Date

Grade

Teacher

Examiner

Level 2 Informal Assessment of Vowel Patterns
(use with Level 2 Vowel Patterns Student Sheets)

I will show you some nonsense words. Read them to me.

2.1 Closed

	Pre-	Post-
fam		
het		
ish		
ot		
nust		
stim		
Score		

2.2 Open

	Pre-	Post-
bo		
li		
mu		
ta		
ne		
vo		
Score		

2.3 Silent *e*

	Pre-	Post-
nake		
fute		
mive		
pere		
stide		
bose		
Score		

2.4 Bossy *r*

	Pre-	Post-
jart		
gorf		
derp		
kird		
murt		
harb		
Score		

2.5 Double Vowel Talkers

	Pre-	Post-
tain		
leep		
poat		
meab		
boe		
tay		
Score		

2.6 Double Vowel Whiners

	Pre-	Post-
mout		
noy		
pown		
voil		
bawp		
goom		
Score		

104

Level 2

Kindergarten–
First Grade

Student Assessment

Sheets

Level 2 Print Awareness: Letter Recognition Student Sheet
2.2 Uppercase

M	S	F	P	A	T
K	B	G	I	N	W
D	J	O	L	C	H
U	R	V	E	Q	Y
X	Z				

2.3 Lowercase

m	s	f	p	a	t
k	b	g	i	n	w
d	j	o	l	c	h
u	r	v	e	q	y
x	z				

Level 2 Synthetic Phonics Student Sheet

2.1 Consonants

m	s	t	d	n
f	p	j	h	g
b	w	l	r	c
k	v	y	q	
x	z			

2.2/2.3 Long and Short Vowels

a	e	i	o	u

2.4 Consonant Digraphs

sh   ch   th   wh   ph

2.5 Consonant Blends

cl   gr   st   bl   sk

2.6 *R*-Controlled Vowels

ar   er   ir   or   ur

Level 2 Synthetic Phonics Student Sheet (continued)

2.7 Vowel Digraphs

ai   ee   oa   oe   ie

2.8 Diphthongs

oy   ow   oi   ou

2.9 Phoneme Segmenting and Blending

Practice item: no

---

me   go   sat   fill   men   nest

Level 2 Analytic Phonics Student Sheet

2.1 Word Families: Matching

Practice item:

fill	Jill	hill	pill	set	hop
fat	mat	cat	zip	met	sat
bit	sit	lit	get	fit	hop
fight	light	might	night	seats	parks
hop	pop	top	man	mop	mom
best	nest	vest	tent	west	belt

Practice item:

hop   top   _____

---

tip   lip   _____

make   bake   _____

sack   pack   _____

bell   tell   _____

dot   hot   _____

bump   jump   _____

Level 2 Analytic Phonics Student Sheet (continued)

2.3 Word Families: Substitution of Initial Letter

Practice item:

| sit | **Change *s* to *b*** | _____ |

| top | **Change *t* to *m*** | _____ |

| lip | **Change *l* to *s*** | _____ |

| car | **Change *c* to *f*** | _____ |

| boat | **Change *b* to *g*** | _____ |

| meet | **Change *m* to *b*** | _____ |

| look | **Change *l* to *b*** | _____ |

| joy | **Change *j* to *t*** | _____ |

Practice item:

sit	**Change *t* to *p***	_____

---

lot	**Change *t* to *g***	_____
pen	**Change *n* to *t***	_____
hip	**Change *p* to *d***	_____
shot	**Change *t* to *p***	_____
plug	**Change *g* to *b***	_____
meet	**Change *m* to *k***	_____

Practice item:

| sit | **Change *i* to *a*** | _____ |

---

make	**Change *a* to *i***	_____
ride	**Change *i* to *o***	_____
wade	**Change *a* to *i***	_____
mud	**Change *u* to *a***	_____
ten	**Change *e* to *i***	_____
stop	**Change *o* to *e***	_____

2.1 Closed

fam	**ot**
het	**nust**
ish	**stim**

2.2 Open

bo	**ta**
li	**ne**
mu	**vo**

2.3 Silent *e*

nake   pere

fute   stide

mive   bose

2.4 Bossy *r*

jart   kird

gorf   murt

derp   harb

2.5 Double Vowel Talkers

tain   meab

leep   boe

poat   tay

2.6 Double Vowel Whiners

mout   voil

noy   bawp

pown   goom

Level 2

Kindergarten–
First Grade

Lesson Plans

Level 2 Prototype Lessons

Level 2 Prototype Lessons

Skill   **Page**

Level 2 Developmental Lessons

The lessons that follow are coded to the previous assessment items. Many different types of children's literature, such as those used for shared reading and guided reading, poems, songs, chants, and stories from home and/or the library are recommended for lessons. For simplicity, however, the following lesson plans are based on only two texts:

Down by the Bay (A traditional song available in the Song Box® series from The Wright Group).

Annabel by Joy Cowley (The Story Basket®, The Wright Group).

These lesson plans are merely examples; teachers should develop their own lessons for whatever literature is planned for the week. Blackline masters are provided in Appendix 1 for use in developing lesson plans.

Level 2 Lesson Plan Format

Book title: *Down by the Bay*		
Process	Materials	Activity
Preread it	Big Book	Do the picture walk. Discuss pictures.
Read it	Big Book	Share the Big Book rhyme by reading it aloud.
Reread it	Big Book	Ask children to join you when they are ready, and then sing the song in an echo format.
Discuss it	Big Book	Ask the students what they noticed about each of the "stories" at the end of the song. Read the first small story and call attention to the rhyming words.
React to it	Big Book	Involve the children in small-group role plays while singing the rhyming stories toward the end of the book. Have small groups make up new rhymes to include in a class Big Book reproduction. Invite the children to create illustrations for the book.
Code it	Following this lesson plan are skill lessons based on this book.	
Apply it		
Transfer it		

Coding lesson: phonological awareness
Skill: rhyming word identification
Title: *Down by the Bay*
Materials: Big Book or poster

Procedures:

1. Review the book the children made using "Did you ever see a *bear*, combing his *hair?*" Review all rhyming words used in their new book.

2. Using the third stanza— "Did you ever see a *bee*, with a sunburned *knee?*"—ask for rhyming words: *bee, knee, three, tree, me, tea, flea.*

3. Use each word to make a new rhyme:
   Did you ever see a bee, sitting in a tree?
   Did you ever see a bee, stinging you or me?
   Did you ever see a bee, serving his friends tea?

4. Repeat with the remaining stanzas.

5. Sing the song from the beginning using the new lyrics.

6. Make a book for each rhyme.

Transfer: Using the book *Annabel,* follow the same basic procedures:

Annabel: *fell, sell, tell, well, dell, yell*

Crocodile: *mile, file, dial, tile*

Baltimore: *tore, for, sore, soar, floor, bore, core*

2.2 Segmenting Words in Sentences

Coding lesson: phonological awareness
Skill: segmenting of words in a sentence
Title: *Down by the Bay*
Materials: Big Book, taped song, Big Book reproduction/innovation

Procedures:

1. Have students clap for each word you say: *bay, say, Kay, Fay, way; bee, me, see, tree, free.*

2. Say *Down by the bay,* clapping for each word. Invite students to join in.

3. Repeat for *Where the watermelons grow.*

4. Sing and clap the words in the song, modeling the first line for students, and having them repeat as an echo.

5. Each day add a stanza. Clap for each word.

Transfer:

1. Using *Annabel,* repeat the activity.

2. Each day add a new stanza.

2.3/2.6 Segmenting and Blending Compound Words

Coding lesson: phonological awareness
Skill: segmenting and blending of compound words
Title: *Down by the Bay*
Materials: Pictures of a watermelon and other compound word items

Procedures:

1. Choose a compound word such as *watermelon*. Show a picture of a watermelon as you say the word *watermelon*. Then cut the picture in half. Say *water* (show the first half), *melon* (show the second half). Invite students to complete the activity with you. Let students say the compound word as a whole and then in parts.

2. Repeat with *sunburn*.

3. Repeat using other words from past stories, songs, or poems.

4. At the completion of the activity, place pictures of compound words on the word wall.

Transfer: Using *Annabel*, repeat the activity for *toothbrush* and *anymore*.

2.4/2.7 Segmenting and Blending Syllables

<table>
<tr><td colspan="1">

Coding lesson: phonological awareness

Skill: segmenting and blending of syllables

Title: *Down by the Bay*

Materials: Picture cards; colored disks, magnetic squares, pop-it blocks, etc.

Procedures:

1. Review with students how to feel how many parts a word has (place your hand under your chin as you say the word).

2. Begin with one-syllable words. Say each word and then have students echo it.

3. Repeat with two-syllable words.

4. Repeat with three-syllable words.

5. Using picture cards cut into two parts, practice saying the whole word, the parts, and then the whole word again.

6. Repeat, using colored discs, magnetic squares, pop-it blocks, etc.

Transfer: Using *Annabel,* repeat the activity:

one-syllable words: *there, once, was, a, she, went, out, bought, new*

two-syllable words: *shopping, shampoo, again, people, wanted*

three-syllable words: *Annabel, crocodile, terrified, Baltimore*

</td></tr>
</table>

2.5/2.7 Segmenting and Blending Phonemes

Coding lesson: phonological awareness
Skill: segmenting and blending of phonemes
Title: *Down by the Bay*
Materials: overhead projector, one-inch tiles; pop-it blocks; tiles, plastic disks

Procedures:

1. Say, *Listen while I say a word:* **by.** *Now listen to the parts:* **b-y.** Place the tiles on the glass of the overhead projector. Say *by.* Say *b-y.* Say *by.*

2. Have students do the same thing at their seats with tiles or plastic disks.

3. Repeat with pop-it blocks. Start with two blocks, pop them apart, and then put them back together.

4. Repeat with other words: *see, bee, bay.*

5. Repeat steps 1–4 with words that have three phonemes: *back, down.*

Transfer: Using *Annabel,* repeat the activity.

two phonemes: *she, out, new, her, in, go, for*

three phonemes: *was, Anna, said, got, girl*

four phonemes: *went, pink, better, train, people*

Coding lesson: phonological awareness
Skill: identification of initial phonemes
Title: *Down by the Bay*
Materials: Big Book

Procedures:

1. Say, *Listen while I say the word **down**. What sound do you hear at the beginning of the word? **/d/**. Say the sound. Now say **down**. Listen for the first sound. Now say **dare**. Listen for the first sound. Now say **did**. Listen for the first sound.*

2. *Let's find all the pictures from the picture book that start like **down, dare**, and **did**.*

3. Make a chart.

4. Take turns pointing to the picture and saying the word.

5. Sing *Down by the Bay* while students sing along. Have students stand up when they hear a word that starts with the /d/ sound. Emphasize /d/ words.

6. Repeat steps 1–5 using other initial sounds.

Transfer: Using *Annabel*, repeat the activity:

/sh/: she, shampoo

/g/: girl, go, got

/w/: was, went, wanted, with, want

/p/: pink, people

2.10 Phoneme Identification: Final

Coding lesson: phonological awareness
Skill: identification of final phonemes
Title: *Down by the Bay*
Materials: Big Book

Procedures:

1. Say, *Listen while I say the word* **melon**. *What sound do you hear at the end of the word?* /n/. *Say the sound. Now say* **melon**. *Listen for the last sound. Now say* **sun**. *Listen for the last sound. Now say* **burn**. *Listen for the last sound.*

2. *Let's find all the pictures from the picture book that end like* **melon, sun, and burn.**

3. Make a chart.

4. Take turns pointing to the picture and saying the word.

5. Sing *Down by the Bay* while students sing along. Have students stand up when they hear a word that ends with /n/. Emphasize these words.

6. Repeat steps 1–5 using other initial sounds.

Transfer: Using *Annabel,* repeat the activity:

/l/:   Annabel, crocodile, people, girl

/t/:   went, out, street, got, start, want

2.11 Phoneme Identification: Medial

Coding lesson: phonological awareness
Skill: identification of medial phonemes
Title: *Down by the Bay*
Materials: Big Book

Procedures:

1. Say, *Listen while I say the word* **moose**. *What sound do you hear in the middle of the word?* **/oo/**. *Say the sound. Now say* **moose**. *Listen for the middle sound. Now say* **goose**. *Listen for the middle sound.*

2. *Let's find all the pictures from the picture book that have a middle sound like* **moose** *and* **goose**.

3. Make a chart.

4. Take turns pointing to the picture and saying the word.

5. Sing *Down by the Bay* while students sing along. Have students stand up when they hear a word with the middle sound **/oo/**. Emphasize these words.

6. Repeat steps 1–5 using other initial sounds.

Transfer: Using *Annabel*, repeat the activity:

/ē/:   people, street

/o/:   bottle, got

2.1 Concepts of Print

Coding lesson: print awareness
Skill: concepts of print familiarity
Title: *Down by the Bay*
Materials: Big Book or poster

Procedures:

1. During the skill segment of the lesson, ask students to

- show you where to start reading
- show you the direction (left to right) of reading
- show you a return sweep
- show you page sequence
- show you words and spaces
- show you top and bottom
- show you words and letters

2. Repeat with posters made by the children, identifying concepts of print in their drawings and in your writing of their rhyming stories: *Did you ever see a _____ ? Down by the Bay.*

Transfer: Using a pointer, have children repeat the skills with other books, posters, reproductions, and innovations around the room.

Coding lesson: print awareness
Skill: recognition of uppercase letters
Title: *Down by the Bay*
Materials: story text; colored transparent tape; wax-covered yarn; clay, shaving cream, etc., for tactile writing

Procedures:

1. Place sentence strips in sentence-strip chart. Ask students to come up one at a time to find
   - all uppercase letters on the page
   - specific uppercase letters embedded in story line

   Ask students to cover the letters with colored transparency tape or circle them with wax-covered yarn.

2. Have students repeat the activity at their desks, completing one sentence strip or one page from the story.

3. Take copies of the letter or letters found to the handwriting center. Have students use clay, shaving cream, glue, puff paint, or sand trays to practice writing the letters.

Transfer: Repeat with Daily News and other songs, stories, and poems around the room.

Coding lesson: print awareness

Skill: recognition of lowercase letters

Title: *Down by the Bay*

Materials: story text; colored transparent tape; wax-covered yarn; clay, shaving cream, etc., for tactile writing

Procedures:

1. Place sentence strips in sentence strip chart. Ask students to come up one at a time to find

- all lowercase letters on the page
- specific lowercase letters embedded in story line

Ask students to cover the letters with colored transparency tape or circle them with wax-covered yarn.

2. Have students repeat the activity at their desks, completing one sentence strip or one page from the story.

3. Take copies of the letter or letters found to the handwriting center. Have students use clay, shaving cream, glue, puff paint, or sand trays to practice writing the letters.

Transfer: Repeat with Daily News and other songs, stories, and poems around the room.

Coding lesson: synthetic phonics
Skill: consonants: sound-symbol association
Title: *Down by the Bay*
Materials: Big Book or poster; reproductions or wall charts around the room; picture charts from phonological awareness activities

Procedures:

These procedures may be repeated with any consonant you are teaching.

In the book *Down by the Bay*, there are many words that begin with *d (down, dare, did, dot)*, *b (bay, back, by, bee, bear)*, and *m (mother, moose, my)*.

1. Have students clap each time they hear a word beginning like *down* as you read the story.

2. Show pictures from the phonological awareness chart of *d* words, asking students to say the words with you while listening for the first sound. Place a magnetic letter card next to each picture as students say the word.

3. Find other words around the room that start with the *d* sound. Review all students' names that begin with *d*, listening for the beginning sound.

4. At the writing center, have students practice writing the letter *d* as they say its sound.

Transfer:

1. Repeat the activity with *b* and *m*.

2. Repeat the activity with another book.

Coding lesson: synthetic phonics
Skill: long vowel: sound-symbol association
Title: *Down by the Bay*
Materials: Big Book or poster; reproductions or wall charts around the room; alphabet cards

Procedures: These procedures may be used with any long vowel you are teaching. In this book, the following long vowel words are used: *my, by, grow, go, say, bay, bee, knee, whale, tail.*

1. Remind students that when they say the letters of the alphabet, the vowels say their own names: *a, e, i, o, u.*

2. Ask students to listen while you say *a, whale, tail.*

3. Ask students to say this with you: *a, a, whale, whale, a, a, tail, tail.* Model saying it and then say it with students.

4. Repeat with *i (by, my), o (go, grow), e (bee, knee).*

5. Ask students to hold up their alphabet cards for the letter *a.* Repeat each word *(whale, tail)* as they hold up the cards. Brainstorm three to five more words and complete the activity.

6. Repeat with long *i, o,* and *e* words and vowel cards.

Transfer: Using *Annabel,* repeat the activity with the following long vowel words:

long *i:* crocodile, terrified

long *e:* people, street

long *o:* go

Coding lesson: synthetic phonics

Skill: short vowel: sound-symbol association

Title: *Down by the Bay*

Materials: Big Book or poster; reproductions or wall charts around the room; picture charts from phonological awareness activities

Procedures: These procedures may be used with any short vowel you are teaching. In this book, the following short vowels are used: *i (did, if, with, kissing, will, his), o (not, dot), e (ever, melons), a (back).*

1. Begin by asking students to listen to you say the vowel *i* followed by *if*. Have students repeat it: *i, if.*

2. Say, *For **if** I do...* and have students clap on the word *if.*

3. Repeat steps 1–2 with the following words and phrases:
 *did, with: **Did** you ever see a whale **with** a polka dot tail?*
 *did, his: **Did** you ever see a bear, combing **his** hair?*
 *will: My mother **will** say...*
 *did, kissing: **Did** you ever see a moose, **kissing** a goose?*

4. Repeat with other short vowels already taught or use the activity with a vowel chart.

Transfer: Repeat the activity with words and phrases from *Annabel* that include short *i:*
*with: She went out shopping **with** her crocodile*
*pink: She bought a bottle of **pink** shampoo.*
*in: The people **in** the street.*

2.4 Consonant Digraphs

Coding lesson: synthetic phonics
Skill: consonant digraphs: sound-symbol association
Title: *Down by the Bay*
Materials: Big Book or poster; reproductions or wall charts around the room; picture charts from phonological awareness activities

Procedures: These procedures may be used with any of the consonant digraphs you are teaching. In this book, the digraph *th* occurs in *the, mother,* and *with.*

1. Show an alphabet card with *th* written on it. Ask students to say the sound. Have students look in the mirror to see and feel the position of their tongues between their teeth. Have students say *this, that, those, there, them.* Each time a student says the sound, have him or her listen to, see, and feel the *th.*

2. Repeat this process using the words *mother* and *with.*

3. Trace the letters *th* in the air as students say each word from the list.

4. Have students clap each time they hear the word *the,* as you read the following:
   Down by the bay (Down by the bay)
   Where the watermelons grow (Where the watermelons grow)

5. Continue, using other phrases from the story that have *th* words in them.

Transfer:

1. Using *Annabel,* repeat the activity for the following words: *there, they,* and *the.*

2. Introduce the digraph *sh* using the following words: *she, shopping, shampoo,* and *toothbrush.*

3. Repeat the activity with words in sentences that you read.

4. Make a digraph wall chart.

Coding lesson: synthetic phonics
Skill: consonant blends: sound-symbol association
Title: *Down by the Bay*
Materials: Big Book or poster; reproductions or wall charts around the room; picture charts from phonological awareness activities; alphabet cards

Procedures: These procedures may be used with any consonant blend you are using. In this book, the blend *gr* occurs in *grow* in "Where the watermelons *grow*."

1. Review with students that a consonant blend means you say both sounds. Practice saying the following words with the *gr* consonant blend: *grow, green, grab, grin, great,* and *grass.*

2. Hold up an alphabet card with *gr* on it as everyone says each of these words.

3. Use each word in a phrase or sentence, holding up the *gr* card as you say the word.

4. Make up an alliteration such as *Great green grass grows so high, I grin as I grab it.*

5. Let students make up their own alliterations.

Transfer:

1. Using *Annabel,* add the following consonant blends: *crocodile, train, toothbrush,* and *street.*

2. Repeat activity with each new consonant blend.

Coding lesson: synthetic phonics
Skill: *r*-controlled vowels: sound-symbol association
Title: *Down by the Bay*
Materials: Big Book or poster; reproductions or wall charts around the room; pictures from the phonological awareness activities.
Procedures: These procedures may be repeated with any r-controlled word you are teaching. With this book, the following words may be used in your lesson: • *er: watermelons, mother, ever, sunburned* • *air: dare, bear, hair* **1.** After students enjoy the story as a song and sing it as an echo, ask them to listen as you say a phrase from the song. Choose phrases that have a number of *r*-controlled words in them. **2.** Ask the students to clap each time they hear an *r*-controlled word. **3.** Say *er, er, er.* Have students repeat *er, er, er.* Say *Watermelons.* Have students repeat. Say *Where the watermelons grow.* Have students repeat, emphasizing the *er* in *watermelons.* Repeat with *mother, ever,* and *sunburned.*

Transfer:

1. Repeat the activity with *air.*

2. Using *Annabel,* repeat the activity with the following *r*-controlled words: *girl, her, better.*

3. Repeat the activity with other *r*-controlled words: *air (terrified), or (anymore, for), ar (start).*

Coding lesson: synthetic phonics

Skill: vowel digraphs: sound-symbol association

Title: *Down by the Bay*

Materials: Big Book or poster; reproductions or wall charts around the room; pictures from the phonological awareness activities; wax-covered yarn; highlight paper

Procedures: These procedures may be repeated with any vowel digraph word you are teaching. With this book, the following words may be used in your lesson: bee, knee, see, bay, say.

1. Write the words on the board that have the *ee* digraph: *bee, knee, see.*

2. Say each word and have the students listen for the *ee* sound.

3. Ask students to come up and circle the *ee* in each word using wax-covered yarn or highlight paper; brainstorm other words they know that have this same sound and spelling such as *fee, tree, free,* and *three.*

4. Using the Big Book, repeat the activity with the *ee* words.

5. After students enjoy the story as a song and participate in singing it as an echo, ask them to listen as you say a phrase from the song. Choose phrases that have a number of *r* words in them. Ask the students to clap each time they hear an *r* word. Say, *er, er, er.* Have students repeat *er, er, er.* Say, *Watermelons.* Have student repeat. Say, *Where the watermelons grow.* Have the students repeat, emphasizing the *er* in *watermelons.*

6. Repeat with *mother, ever,* and *sunburned.*

Transfer: Repeat the activity with *Annabel* for *ee* (street), *ai* (train. again, gain), and *ie* (terrified. fied).

2.8 Vowel Diphthongs

Coding lesson: synthetic phonics
Skill: vowel diphthongs: sound-symbol association
Title: *Down by the Bay*
Materials: Big Book; poster; reproductions or wall charts around the room; red markers or crayons
Procedures: These procedures may be used with any of the vowel diphthongs you are teaching. The ones found in this book are *ow (down)* and *oo (moose, goose)*. 1. Write *ow* and *down* on the board. Have a student come to the board to circle the *ow* in *down*. Repeat the activity with the phrase *Down by the bay, down by the bay.* Repeat it with the entire book. Duplicate the pages for each child. Have them trace over the *ow* in red so it is easy to see. 2. Make a list of other words with the same pattern such as *gown* and *town.* 3. Repeat the activity with the *oo* pattern vowel diphthong.
Transfer: 1. Using *Annabel,* locate other diphthongs: *ou* (out); *aw* (bought). 2. Repeat the activity with *ou* and *aw.*

Coding lesson: synthetic phonics
Skill: phoneme segmenting and blending
Title: *Down by the Bay*
Materials: Big Book; poster; reproductions and/or wall products in the room

Procedures: These procedures can be used with any phoneme blending sequence you are teaching. In this book, the words that should be used are the following: *by, bee, bay, say, knee, do, back, down, sun, did.*

Say, *Say this word.* (**by**) *Now sound it out.* (**/b/ /ī/**) *Now say the whole word again.* (**by**)

Transfer:

Using *Annabel,* practice phoneme blending on the following words:

new (/n/ /oo/), *Anna* (/a/ /n/ /u/), *go* (/g/ /ō/), *she* (/sh/ /ē/), *if* (/i/ /f/), *got* (/g/ /o/ /t/).

Coding lesson: analytic phonics
Skill: matching word families
Title: *Down by the Bay*
Materials: Big Book; poster; reproduction and/or wall products in the classroom; transparencies and overhead projector; wax-covered yarn; colored markers

Procedures: These procedures may be used with any of the word families you are teaching. The word families used in this book are: *ay (bay)*, *own (down)*, *ack (back)*, and *ill (will)*.

1. Make a list of familiar words from each word family, such as the following:

bay	down	back	will
Fay	brown	sack	pill
day	town	lack	dill
pay	clown	tack	fill
say	frown	Mack	bill
clay	gown	pack	till
may			sill

2. Using an overhead projector, write each word from a single word family on the transparency. Have students find the same words on their papers and color code the patterns you model. Repeat the activity for each pattern. Then find that pattern in the book and circle it with a piece of wax-covered yarn.

Transfer: Using Annabel, repeat the activity with these patterns: *all (call)*, *op (shop)*, *ink (pink)*, *ew (new)*, *ot (got)*, *ought (bought)*, *ith (with)*, *art (start)*.

2.2 Word Families: Production

Coding lesson: analytic phonics
Skill: production of word families
Title: *Down by the Bay*
Materials: Big Book; poster; reproduction and/or wall charts; sticky notes

Procedures:

1. Write one of the word families found in this book, such as *ay*, on the board.

2. After you have written two words from the word family, ask a student to come up and add a new word.

3. Point to the words created by the students and ask them how they are the same.

4. Ask a student to cover the pattern *ay* with a sticky note. Repeat with each word in the pattern. Use each word in a sentence. Highlight the word and then the pattern. Find words of the same family on the wall charts or word walls.

5. Repeat with other patterns in the book.

6. Reread a page of the story that includes the pattern so that the students can find the pattern embedded in text.

Transfer: Repeat the activity with the patterns found in a new Big Book such as *Annabel: all (call), ought (bought), or (for)*.

2.3 Word Families: Substitution of Initial Letter

Coding lesson: analytic phonics
Skill: substitution of an initial letter
Title: *Down by the Bay*
Materials: Big Book; poster and/or reproduction or other wall charts; colored markers
Procedures: **1.** Choose one of the word families from prior lessons, such as *ay.* **2.** Write the word *bay* on the board. Show the students that when you change the *b* to *d*, the word becomes *day*. Ask students to change the *d* in *day* to *s*. What is the new word? *(Say).* **3.** Give the students a new beginning letter such as *p*. Ask them to add *ay* and tell you the new word. **4.** Repeat with the other word families in this book. **5.** Add these new words to the word wall or begin a new chart of word families. **6.** Give students a chance to color code all the patterns. **7.** Find the patterns in the story. Practice reading a sentence with the students, pointing to the patterned word as you read. **8.** Invite a student to lead the other students in the same activity. **9.** Provide students with a copy of one page of print from the story. Have them visually track for all words with a certain pattern.
Transfer: Repeat the activity with a Big Book such as *Annabel.* The following word families may be used with these activities: *all (call), ought (bought), ink (pink), ew (new), or (for),* and *art (start).*

2.4 Word Families: Substitution of Final Letter

Coding lesson: analytic phonics
Skill: substitution of the final letter
Title: *Down by the Bay*
Materials: Big Book; reproduction and/or other wall charts

Procedures:

1. Choose a word family from the book. Write one word from the family on the chalkboard, such as *his*.

2. *Take off the s from **his** and that leaves **hi**. If I put in the letter **t**, the word becomes **hit**. Take away the t, and write the letter p. Now the word is **hip**.*

3. Ask a student to circle in red the last letter in these words: *his, hit, hip*.

4. Ask students how many words you can make by changing the last letter.

5. Repeat with other word families found in the story.

Transfer: Using another Big Book such as *Annabel,* repeat the activity with other word patterns such as *for* and *in*.

2.5 Word Families: Substitution of Middle Letter

Coding lesson: analytic phonics
Skill: substitution of a middle letter
Title: *Down by the Bay*
Materials: Big Book; song book; reproduction and/or other wall charts

Procedures: These activities can be used to teach the substitution of the medial sound/letter of any words to make new words. For this book, the following words may be selected: *not, will, his, did.*

1. Write the word *not* on the board. Ask the students to observe what the new word is when the middle letter *o* is removed and replaced with the middle letter *e. The new word is* **net.** *Take the* **e** *out and put a* **u** *there, and the new word is* **nut.**

2. Repeat the process with the following words: will, well, wall; his, has; did, dad, dud.

3. Use each new word in a sentence.

4. Find the first word of each pattern (*not, will, his,* and *did*) in the story.

Transfer: Using *Annabel,* repeat the activity with the following words: *for, pink, bell.*

2.1 Vowel Patterns: Closed

Coding lesson: vowel patterns
Skill: recognition of the closed vowel pattern (a word or syllable that contains only one vowel and is followed by one or more consonants)
Title: *Down by the Bay*
Materials: Big Book or poster; copy of text on transparency; overhead projector; paper copy of text for each student; vowel pattern chart on magnetic board; rainbow alphabet (color-coded paper clips)

Procedures:

1. Model finding the CVC (consonant - vowel - consonant) pattern words like *back* on the transparency.

2. Have students code the vowel in red as they repeat the closed vowel pattern jingle: *One lonely vowel squished in the middle says its special sound just a little.*

3. Give a word card to a student to put on the magnetic wall chart.

4. Repeat with *not, will, did, his, sun, with, kiss.*

5. Make each word with the rainbow alphabet.

Transfer: Repeat the activity with other charts, books, and songs

Coding lesson: vowel patterns

Skill: recognition of the open vowel pattern (a word or syllable that ends with one vowel that is long)

Title: *Down by the Bay*

Materials: Big Book or poster; paper copy of text for each student; vowel pattern chart on magnetic board; rainbow alphabet (color-coded paper clips)

Procedures:

1. Review the following jingle: *If one vowel at the end is free, it pops way up and says its name to me.*

2. Ask the students to code each vowel in words that fit the pattern *(by, go, my)* by tracing over the vowel in red.

3. Give a student a word card with the coded vowel. Ask the student to place it on the magnetic board under the open vowel heading.

4. Repeat with each word. Have students make the words with the rainbow alphabet.

5. Have students write the words on their own vowel pattern charts.

6. Have students come up and circle the open vowel pattern words in the Big Book with their hands.

Transfer:

1. Using *Annabel,* repeat the activity with the following open vowel pattern words: *she, go.*

2. See how many other open words the students can find around the room.

Coding lesson: vowel patterns

Skill: recognition of the silent *e* vowel pattern (a word or syllable that has a vowel followed by a silent *e*)

Title: *Down by the Bay*

Materials: Big Book or poster; paper copy of text for each student; vowel pattern chart on magnetic board; rainbow alphabet (color-coded paper clips)

Procedures:

1. Tell students, *The magic e is so powerful, it gives all its strength to the other vowel so that that vowel can say its real name. Since it gives away all its power, the final e is silent.*

2. Have students use red markers to visually track on their text copies to find any silent *e* pattern words. The words that follow the silent *e* pattern in this book are *home* and *whale.* Have them trace over the vowel in red, write the word on their own charts, and make the word with the rainbow alphabet.

3. Have students place their words on magnetic word cards on the magnetic vowel chart. After all words have been placed on the chart, ask students to use their word in a sentence and then find it in the book. Read the sentence from the book and point to the silent *e* words.

Transfer: Using *Annabel,* repeat the activity with the following silent *e* words from that book: *crocodile, more, anymore.*

2.4 Vowel Patterns: Bossy r

Coding lesson: vowel patterns
Skill: recognition of bossy *r* vowel pattern (a word or syllable containing a vowel followed by *r* in which the vowel sound is altered by the *r*)
Title: *Down by the Bay*
Materials: Big Book; paper copy of text for each student; vowel pattern chart on magnetic board; rainbow alphabet

Procedures:

1. Select a bossy *r* word from the story, such as *bear*. Tell students, *The letter r is so bossy that it won't let the vowel say its short (special) or long (real name) sound, but must say the /r/ sound, as in* **car**.

2. Have students color code the vowels and the *r* in red.

3. Have students take the magnetic card with the word *bear* on it and place it in the proper box on the magnetic board. Ask the other students if it has been placed correctly.

4. Have all students find the word on their papers, outline the vowels in red, and use their rainbow alphabet to form the pattern on their desks.

5. Have the students repeat the process with the following words: *hair, ever, water.*

6. Find each of these words in the story. Make up sentences using these words in new ways.

Transfer: Repeat the activity with the following patterned words from *Annabel: her, terrified, for, more.*

2.5 Vowel Patterns: Double Vowel Talkers

Coding lesson: vowel patterns
Skill: recognition of the double vowel talker pattern (a word or syllable containing two adjacent vowels, the first of which is long)
Title: *Down by the Bay*
Materials: Big Book; copy of text on transparency; overhead projector; paper copy of text for each student; vowel pattern chart on magnetic board; rainbow alphabet

Procedures:

1. Review the double vowel talker pattern jingle: *When two vowels go walking, the first one does the talking—and says its name.*

2. After you model the procedure on the transparency, have students trace in red marker the double vowels in the following words from the book: *bay, say, see, bee, knee, tail.*

3. Give students a copy of each of the words on magnetic cards to place on the classroom vowel pattern chart.

4. Ask students to make each word with their rainbow alphabet and write the words on their paper copies of the chart.

5. Ask the students to find each of these words in their text copies and circle them.

Transfer: Using *Annabel,* repeat the activity with the following words from the story that have the double vowel talker pattern: *street, train, again.*

2.6 Vowel Patterns: Double Vowel Whiners

Coding lesson: vowel patterns
Skill: recognition of the double vowel whiner pattern (a word or syllable that contains two adjacent vowels that do not say their long or short sounds but whine a very different sound)
Title: *Down by the Bay*
Materials: Big Book; copy of text on transparency; overhead projector; paper copy of text for each student; vowel pattern chart on magnetic board; rainbow alphabet
Procedures: 1. On the transparency, model finding the words from this story that have the double vowel whiner pattern. The words in this book that fit this pattern are: down, moose, goose, you. Tell the students, *Sometimes, when two vowels are next to each other, they make a funny whining sound, like when you fall down and say, "Ow," "Aw," "Oy," or "Boo-hoo."* 2. Starting with the word *down*, have the students trace the *ow* with their red marking pens and then place the correct magnetic card on the classroom magnetic vowel pattern chart. 3. Repeat with the other words from this book. Have students make each word with the rainbow alphabet and then write the word in the correct box on their charts. Use each word in a sentence. 4. Ask students to locate each word on their copies of the text and circle it. 5. Have students find other double vowel whiners and include them on their charts.
Transfer: Using *Annabel*, repeat the activity using the words in that story that have the double vowel whiner pattern: *out, bought, new.*

Level 3

First Grade-
Second Grade

Teacher's Assessment

Sheets

Level 3 Developmental Assessment and Instructional Matrix

Assessment Component	Subtests
Phonological Awareness	**3.1 Rhyming Words**
	3.2 Segmenting: Words in Sentences
	3.3 Segmenting: Compound Words
	3.4 Segmenting: Syllables
	3.5 Segmenting: Phonemes
	3.6 Blending: Compound Words
	3.7 Blending Syllables
	3.8 Blending: Phonemes
	3.9 Phoneme Identification: Initial
	3.10 Phoneme Identification: Final
	3.11 Phoneme Identification: Medial
	3.12 Manipulation: Deletion
	3.13 Manipulation: Substitutions: Initial
	3.14 Manipulation: Substitutions: Final
	3.15 Manipulation: Substitutions: Medial

Print Awareness	3.1 Concepts of Print
	3.2 Letter Recognition: Uppercase
	3.3 Letter Recognition: Lowercase
	3.4 Letter Recognition: Blends
	3.5 Letter Recognition: Digraphs
Synthetic Phonics	3.1 Consonants
	3.2 Long Vowels
	3.3 Short Vowels
	3.4 Consonant Digraphs
	3.5 Consonant Blends
	3.6 *R*-controlled Vowels
	3.7 Vowel Digraphs
	3.8 Diphthongs
	3.9 Phoneme Segmenting and Blending
Analytic Phonics	3.2 Word Families: Production
	3.3 Word Families: Substitution of Initial Letter
	3.4 Word Families: Substitution of Final Letter
	3.5 Word Families: Substitution of Middle Letter

Vowel Patterns	3.1 Closed (VC, CVC)
	3.2 Open
	3.3 Silent *e*
	3.4 Bossy *r*
	3.5 Double Vowel Talkers
	3.6 Double Vowel Whiners
	3.7 C + *le*
Structural Analysis	3.1 Root Words
	3.2 Affixes: Suffixes
	3.3 Affixes: Prefixes
	3.4 Compound Words
	3.5 Contractions
	3.6 Syllabication: C + *le*
	3.7 Syllabication: VC/CV
	3.8 Syllabication: V/CV
	3.9 Syllabication: VC/V

Level 3 Student Profile

Phonological Awareness

Subtest	Pre-	Post-
3.1		
3.2		
3.3		
3.4		
3.5		
3.6		
3.7		
3.8		
3.9		
3.10		
3.11		
3.12		
3.13		
3.14		
3.15		

Print Awareness

Subtest	Pre-	Post-
3.1		
3.2		
3.3		
3.4		
3.5		

Synthetic Phonics

Subtest	Pre-	Post-
3.1		
3.2		
3.3		
3.4		
3.5		
3.6		
3.7		
3.8		
3.9		

Analytic Phonics

Subtest	Pre-	Post-
3.2		
33		
3.4		
3.5		
3.6		

Vowel Patterns

Subtest	Pre-	Post-
3.1		
3.2		
3.3		
3.4		
3.5		
3.6		

Structural Analysis

Subtest	Pre-	Post-
3.1		
3.2		
3.3		
3.4		
3.5		
3.6		
3.7		
3.8		
3.9		

Name		
Grade	Teacher	
Examiner		Date

Level 3 Informal Assessment of
Phonological Awareness

Date

Name

Grade   Teacher

Examiner

Directions: Mark a + for a correct response and a – for an incorrect response. Each subtest has a practice item. The words the teacher says are in italics. A passing score is 4 correct responses out of 6. If a student misses two or more items, instruction may be indicated. Correct responses are in parentheses.

Level 3 Informal Assessment of Phonological Awareness

3.1   Rhyming Words

Say "yes" if the words rhyme and "no" if they don't rhyme. Do these words rhyme? **pin, fin** (yes)

hat, pat (yes)	_____	**sun, run** (yes)	_____
man, can (yes)	_____	**lamp, land** (no)	_____
chair, floor (no)	_____	**clock, block** (yes)	_____

3.2   Segmenting: Words in Sentences

Clap your hands each time you hear a word: **Come to my house.** (4 claps)

I have a dog. (4 claps)		_____
The floor was wet and cold. (6 claps)		_____
The cat ran up the hill. (6 claps)		_____
My house has a pool. (5 claps)		_____
Tigers are big and strong. (5 claps)		_____
The baseball is round. (4 claps)		_____

3.3   Segmenting: Compound Words

I'm going to say a word that has two parts. Listen while I say it:

sunshine. *Now tell me each part.* (sun - shine)

milkshake	_____	**fireman**	_____
railroad	_____	**houseboat**	_____
doghouse	_____	**toothbrush**	_____

Level 3 Informal Assessment of
Phonological Awareness (continued)

Directions: Mark a + for a correct response and a – for an incorrect response.

Name		Date
Grade	Teacher	
Examiner		

Level 3 Informal Assessment of Phonological Awareness
(continued)

3.4 *Segmenting: Syllables*

Listen while I say a word: **pencil**. *Now say the word and clap your*

hands for each part you hear. (2 claps)

table (2 claps) _____   **picture** (2 claps) _____

chair (1 clap) _____   **bottle** (2 claps) _____

grass (1 clap) _____   **radio** (3 claps) _____

3.5 *Segmenting: Phonemes*

I will say a word: **mat.** *Tell me each sound you hear in* **mat.**

Say /m/ - /a/ - /t/ with the student.

see (s - ee) _____   **ship** (sh - i - p) _____

do (d - oo) _____   **side** (s - i - d) _____

fat (f - a - t) _____   **city** (s - i - t - ee) _____

3.6 *Blending: Compound Words*

Listen while I say two words: **mail, box**. *Now say them together.*

cup - cake _____   **black - board** _____

some - thing _____   **blue - jay** _____

air - port _____   **space - man** _____

3.7 *Blending: Syllables*

Listen while I say two word parts: **bas - ket**. *Now say them together.*

ti - ger _____   **sta - tion** _____

cir - cus _____   **el - e - phant** _____

ea - gle _____   **ta - ble** _____

Level 3 Informal Assessment of Phonological Awareness (continued)

Directions: Mark a + for a correct response and a – for an incorrect response.

Name		Date
Grade	Teacher	
Examiner		

Level 3 Informal Assessment of Phonological Awareness (continued)

3.8 Blending: Phonemes

Listen while I say some sounds: /a/ - /t/. Now say them together.

m - e	_____	s - ea - t	_____
s - o	_____	d - o - g	_____
f - i - sh	_____	l - u - n - ch	_____

3.9 Phoneme Identification: Initial

Listen to the beginning sound in the word **soap.** *Say the beginning sound in the word* **soap.**

milk	____	vacuum	____
fish	____	nest	____
zoo	____	suit	____

3.10 Phoneme Identification: Final

Listen to the ending sound in the word **bus.** *Tell me the ending sound.*

top	_____	duck	_____
pit	_____	come	_____
mug	_____	house	_____

3.11 Phoneme Identification: Medial

Listen to the middle sound in the word **meet.** *Tell me the middle sound.*

cake	_____	pat	_____
boat	_____	him	_____
ride	_____	set	_____

Level 3 Informal Assessment of
Phonological Awareness (continued)

Directions: Mark a + for a correct response and a – for an incorrect response.

Name		Date
Grade	Teacher	
Examiner		

Level 3 Informal Assessment of Phonological Awareness
(continued)

3.12 Manipulation: Deletion

Say the word **football.** *Say it again but don't say* **foot.** *Say* ball *with the*

student.

    Say the word **houseboat.** Say it again but don't say **house.** (boat) _____

    Say the word **tiger.** Say it again but don't say **ti.** (ger)   _____

    Say the word **coat.** Say it again but don't say **c.** (oat)   _____

    Say the word **billboard.** Say it again but don't say **board.** (bill)   _____

    Say the word **table.** Say it again but don't say **ble.** (ta)   _____

    Say the word **soup.** Say it again but don't say **p.** (sou)   _____

3.13 Manipulation: Substitutions: Initial

Listen while I say the word **hen.** *If I change the* /**h**/ *to* /**p**/, *the new*

word is **pen.** *Now say the word* mat. *Change the* /**m**/ *to* /**s**/.

The new word is _____. (sat)

    Say **hill.** Change the /**h**/ to /**j**/. (Jill)   _____

    Say **fun.** Change the /**f**/ to /**s**/. (sun)   _____

    Say **might.** Change the /**m**/ to /**f**/. (fight)   _____

    Say **pay.** Change the /**p**/ to /**d**/. (day)   _____

    Say **sit.** Change the /**s**/ to /**f**/. (fit)   _____

    Say **hop.** Change the /**h**/ to /**t**/. (top)   _____

Level 3 Phonological Awareness Informal Assessment (continued)

Directions: Mark a + for a correct response and a – for an incorrect response.

Name		Date
Grade	Teacher	
	Examiner	

Level 3 Informal Assessment of Phonological Awareness (continued)

3.14 Manipulation: Substitutions: Final

Listen while I say the word **hop.** *If I change the /p/ to /g/, the new word is* **hog.** *Now say the word* **sat.** *Change the /t/ to /k/. The new word is _____.* (sack)

Say **cut.** Change the /t/ to /f/. (cuff) _____

Say **like.** Change the /k/ to /t/. (light) _____

Say **bait.** Change the /t/ to /k/. (bake) _____

Say **plum.** Change the /m/ to /s/. (plus) _____

Say **mop.** Change the /p/ to /m/. (mom) _____

Say **cat.** Change the /t/ to /p/. (cap) _____

3.15 Manipulation: Substitutions: Medial

Listen while I say the word **mate.** *If I change the /a/ to /i/, the new word is* **might.** *Now say the word* **seep.** *Change the /ee/ to /oa/. The new word is _____.* (soap)

Say **pet.** Change the /e/ to /i/. (pit) _____

Say **cab.** Change the /a/ to /o/. (cob) _____

Say **fit.** Change the /i/ to /a/. (fat) _____

Say **moon.** Change the /oo/ to /ee/. (mean) _____

Say **beat.** Change the /ea/ to /i/. (bite) _____

Say **mop.** Change the /o/ to /a/ (map) _____

164

Level 3 Informal Assessment of Print Awareness (Concepts of Print Checklist)

Purpose

The purpose of the Concepts of Print Assessment is to help you evaluate students' understanding of the details of print as well as related behaviors. Emergent learners must completely grasp the concepts of print to experience success in reading. This checklist is designed to help familiarize you with these concepts so that you will know what to look for when observing students on a daily basis.

When to Use

Use the Concepts of Print Assessment as an ongoing observational tool at the beginning of the year and then quarterly to record and monitor students' growth in understanding print concepts.

How to Use

Prior to using this assessment, familiarize yourself with the types of tasks required on the checklist. Assess each child individually. Provide the student with a book that is somewhat familiar; using a familiar book is more meaningful to students.

Read through the book, either together or with the student reading independently. During the reading, record your observations of the student's behaviors. Try writing with a different color each time you use the assessment to make the student's record easier to track.

Several of the tasks on the Concepts of Print Assessment are also observable during shared reading, guided reading, and writing, and at other times throughout the day. As you observe a student demonstrating proficiency with a task, make a note of it to record later.

Scoring and Informing Instruction

A total of 23 items are assessed on the Concepts of Print Assessment. Score each item as follows:

+ = Understands concept (answers the question or performs the indicated behavior without hesitation)

√ = Needs review (answers the question or performs the indicated behavior with hesitation or with additional prompting)

– = Does not understand concept (cannot answer the question or perform the indicated behavior)

In addition, write down any comments that reflect the student's print behaviors.

Name _____ **Date** _____

Grade _____ **Teacher** _____

Examiner _____

Directions: Have the student read through a familiar book. During the reading, record your observations of the student's behaviors.

Level 3 Print Awareness: Concepts of Print Checklist

Assess	Prompt the Student	Pre-	Post-	Comments
Book Concepts				
Cover of book	Show me how you hold a book.			
	Show me the front of the book.			
	Show me the name of the author/illustrator.			
	Show me the back of the book.			
Title	Show me the title.			
Title page	Show me the title page.			
Text Concepts				
Print tells a story	Where does the book tell the story?			
Concept of a word	Can you put your fingers around a word?			
	Can you find two words that are the same?			
	Where is the first word on this page?			
	Where is the last word on this page?			
Concept of letter	Can you put your fingers around a letter?			
	Can you tell me the names of some letters on this page?			

+ = Understands concept (answers the question or performs the indicated behavior without hesitation)

√ = Needs review (answers the question or performs the indicated behavior with hesitation or with additional prompting)

− = Does not understand concept (cannot answer the question or perform the indicated behavior)

Level 3 Print Awareness: Concepts of Print Checklist
(continued)

Assess	Prompt the Student	Pre-	Post-	Comments
Directionality				
Starting at beginning of book, finishing at end of book	Which page do we read first? Which page do we read last?			
Top to bottom of page	Show me where you start reading on this page.			
Left-to-right in sentence	Which way do we go when we're reading?			
Return sweep	Where do we go when we get to the end of the line?			
Left-to-right page sequence	Where do we go when we finish reading a page?			
One-to-one Correspondence	Read this sentence and point to each word as you read.			
	Did what you read match the number of words?			
Mechanics				
Capital letter	Can you find a capital letter?			
Lowercase letter	Can you find a small or lowercase letter?			
Period (.)	What is this mark called? What do you do when you see it?			
Comma (,)	What is this mark called? What do you do when you see it?			
Question mark (?)	What is this mark called? What does it mean?			
Exclamation mark (!)	What is this mark called? What does it mean?			
Quotation marks (" ")	What are these marks called? What do they mean?			
Score				

Level 3 Print Awareness: Concepts of Print Checklist (continued)

Directions: Have the student read through a familiar book. During the reading, record your observations of the student's behaviors.

Name		Date
Grade	Teacher	
Examiner		

Directions: Have the student point to each capital letter and name it. Repeat with the lowercase letters. Mark a + for a correct response and a – for an incorrect response.

Name		Date
Grade	Teacher	
Examiner		

Level 3 Print Awareness: Letter Recognition Score Sheet
(use with Level 3 Print Awareness: Letter Recognition Student Sheets)

3.2 Uppercase

Letter	Pre-	Post-
M		
S		
F		
P		
A		
T		
K		
B		
G		
I		
N		
W		
D		
J		
O		
L		
C		
H		
U		
R		
V		
E		
Q		
Y		
X		
Z		
Score		

3.3 Lowercase

Letter	Pre-	Post-
m		
s		
f		
p		
a		
t		
k		
b		
g		
i		
n		
w		
d		
j		
o		
l		
c		
h		
u		
r		
v		
e		
q		
y		
x		
z		
Score		

Comments:

Confusions:

Unknown letters:

Level 3 Print Awareness: Letter Recognition Score Sheet
(continued)

(use with Level 3 Print Awareness: Letter Recognition Student Sheets)

3.4 Digraphs

Circle the digraph in the following words.

	Pre-	Post-
(sh)op		
(wh)ale		
(th)is		
fi(sh)		
(ch)alk		
lun(ch)		
Score		

3.5 Blends

Circle the blend in the following words.

	Pre-	Post-
(bl)ock		
(sk)ate		
(gr)een		
sa(nd)		
fa(st)		
(pl)ay		
Score		

Level 3 Print Awareness: Letter Recognition Score Sheet (continued)

Directions: Mark a + for a correct response and a – for an incorrect response.

Name		Date
Grade	Teacher	
Examiner		

Level 3 Informal Assessment of Synthetic Phonics

Directions: Mark a + for a correct response and a – for an incorrect response.

		Date
Name		
Grade	Teacher	
	Examiner	

Level 3 Informal Assessment of Synthetic Phonics
(use with Level 3 Synthetic Phonics Student Sheets)

3.1 Consonants

Ask the student to point to each letter on the Student Sheet and tell you the sound each consonant makes. For the letters *g* and *c*, ask if the student knows another sound the letter makes.

Example: b (/*b*/)

	Pre-	Post-
m (/m/)		
s (/s/)		
t (/t/)		
d (/d/)		
n (/n/)		
f (/f/)		
p (/p/)		
j (/j/)		
h (/h/)		
g (/g/)		
g (/j/)		
b (/b/)		
w (/w/)		
l (/l/)		
r (/r/)		
c (/k/)		
c (/s/)		
k (/k/)		
v (/v/)		
y (/y/)		
q (/kw/)		
x (/ks/)		
z (/z/)		
Score		

3.2/3.3 Long and Short Vowels

Ask the student to look at each letter and tell you the sound it makes. Enter the response in the appropriate column, Long or Short. Then ask if the student knows another sound the letter makes.

	Pre-		Post-	
	Long	Short	Long	Short
a				
e				
i				
o				
u				
Score				

170

Level 3 Informal Assessment of Synthetic Phonics (continued)

(use with Level 3 Synthetic Phonics Student Sheets)

Look at these letters. Tell me what sounds they make.

Example: st

3.4 Consonant Digraphs
3.5 Consonant Blends

	Pre-	Post-
sh		
ch		
th		
wh		
ph		
cl		
gr		
st		
bl		
sk		
Score		

3.7 Vowel Digraphs

	Pre-	Post-
ai (/ā/)		
ee (/ē/)		
oa (/ō/)		
oe (/ō/)		
ie (/ē/)		
Score		

3.8 Diphthongs

	Pre-	Post-
oy (/oy/)		
ow (/ow/)		
oi (/oi/)		
ou (/ou/)		
Score		

2.6 *R*-Controlled Vowels

	Pre-	Post-
ar (/ar/)		
er (/er/)		
ir (/er/)		
or (/or/)		
ur (/er/)		
Score		

3.9 Phoneme Segmenting and Blending

Sound it out. Now say the whole word.

	Pre-	Post-
m - e (me)		
g - o (go)		
s - a - t (sat)		
f - i - l (fill)		
m - e - n (men)		
n - e - s - t (nest)		
Score		

171

Name		
Grade	Teacher	
Examiner		Date

Level 3 Informal Assessment of Analytic Phonics

Date

Name

Teacher

Grade

Examiner

Directions: Mark a + for a correct response and a – for an incorrect response.

Level 3 Informal Assessment of Analytic Phonics
(use with Level 3 Analytic Phonics Student Sheets)

3.2 Word Families: Production

Write another word in the same word family as **hop** *and* **top**. *(pop)*
Add to these word families.

	Pre-	Post-
tip, lip		
make, bake		
sack, pack		
bell, tell		
dot, hot		
bump, jump		
Score		

3.3 Word Families: Substitution of Initial Letter

Show the student the word **sit**. *Look at the word* **sit**.
Change the first letter **s** *to* **b**. *Say the new word* (bit) *and*
write it on the line.

			Pre-	Post-
top	Change *t* to *m*	(mop)		
lip	Change *l* to *s*	(sip)		
car	Change *c* to *f*	(far)		
boat	Change *b* to *g*	(goat)		
meet	Change *m* to *b*	(beet)		
look	Change *l* to *b*	(book)		
joy	Change *j* to *t*	(toy)		
Score				

172

Level 3 Informal Assessment of Analytic Phonics (continued)

Directions: Mark a + for a correct response and a – for an incorrect response.

Name		Date
Grade	Teacher	
Examiner		

Level 3 Informal Assessment of Analytic Phonics (continued)

(use with Level 3 Analytic Phonics Student Sheets)

3.4 Word Families: Substitution of Final Letter

Show student the word **sit**. *Look at the word **sit**. Change the last letter to **p**. Say the new word* (sip) *and write it on the line.*

			Pre-	Post-
lot	Change *t* to *g*	(got)		
pen	Change *n* to *t*	(pet)		
hip	Change *p* to *d*	(hid)		
shot	Change *t* to *p*	(shop)		
plug	Change *g* to *s*	(plus)		
meet	Change *t* to *k*	(meek)		
Score				

3.5 Word Families: Substitution of Medial Letter

Show student the word **sit**. *Look at the word **sit**. Change the middle letter to **a**. Say the new word* (sat) *and write it on the line.*

			Pre-	Post-
make	Change *a* to *i*	(mike)		
ride	Change *i* to *o*	(rode)		
wade	Change *a* to *i*	(wide)		
mud	Change *u* to *a*	(mad)		
ten	Change *e* to *i*	(tin)		
stop	Change *o* to *e*	(step)		
Score				

Level 3 Informal Assessment of Vowel Patterns

Directions: Mark a + for a correct response and a – for an incorrect response.

Name		Date
Grade	Teacher	
Examiner		

Level 3 Informal Assessment of Vowel Patterns
(refer to Level 3 Vowel Patterns Student Sheets)

I will show you some nonsense words. Read them to me.

3.1 Closed

	Pre-	Post-
fam		
het		
ish		
ot		
nust		
stim		
Score		

3.2 Open

	Pre-	Post-
bo		
li		
mu		
ta		
ne		
vo		
Score		

3.3 Silent *e*

	Pre-	Post-
nake		
fute		
mive		
pere		
stide		
bose		
Score		

3.4 Bossy *r*

	Pre-	Post-
jart		
gorf		
derp		
kird		
murt		
harb		
Score		

3.5 Double Vowel Talkers

	Pre-	Post-
tain		
leep		
poat		
meab		
boe		
tay		
Score		

3.6 Double Vowel Whiners

	Pre-	Post-
mout		
noy		
pown		
voil		
bawp		
goom		
Score		

3.7 Consonant + *le*

	Pre-	Post-
caple		
durkle		
pubble		
rizzle		
hottle		
tifle		
Score		

Level 3 Informal Assessment of Structural Analysis

(refer to Level 3 Structural Analysis Student Sheets)

3.1 Root Words

Box in the root word of **runs.** (run)

		Pre-	Post-
friendly	(friend)		
turning	(turn)		
talking	(talk)		
playful	(play)		
buttons	(button)		
heated	(heat)		
Score			

3.3 Affixes: Prefixes

Box in the prefix of the word **dislike.** (dis)

		Pre-	Post-
replay	(re)		
unable	(un)		
preview	(pre)		
rewrite	(re)		
unhappy	(un)		
disappear	(dis)		
Score			

3.2 Affixes: Suffixes

Box in the suffix of the word **airplanes.** (s)

		Pre-	Post-
pets	(s)		
books	(s)		
walked	(ed)		
wanted	(ed)		
talking	(ing)		
playing	(ing)		
Score			

Level 3 Informal Assessment of Structural Analysis

Directions: Mark a + for a correct response and a – for an incorrect response.

Name		Date
Grade	Teacher	
Examiner		

Level 3 Informal Assessment of Structural Analysis (continued)

Directions: Mark a + for a correct response and a – for an incorrect response.

Name	Date
Grade	**Teacher**
	Examiner

Level 3 Informal Assessment of Structural Analysis (continued)

(refer to Level 3 Structural Analysis Student Sheets)

3.4 Compound Words

Look at the compound word **milkshake**. *Draw a line between the two parts.* (milk/shake)

		Pre-	Post-
sunshine	(sun/shine)		
doghouse	(dog/house)		
railroad	(rail/road)		
outside	(out/side)		
fireman	(fire/man)		
blackboard	(black/board)		
Score			

3.6 Syllabication: C + *le*

Divide this word into syllables: **apple**. (ap/ple)

		Pre-	Post-
table	(ta/ble)		
bubble	(bub/ble)		
purple	(pur/ple)		
rifle	(ri/fle)		
cycle	(cy/cle)		
puddle	(pud/dle)		
Score			

3.5 Contractions

Write the contraction for the words **can not**. (can't)

		Pre-	Post-
he is	(he's)		
let us	(let's)		
we will	(we'll)		
is not	(isn't)		
I am	(I'm)		
did not	(didn't)		
Score			

176

(refer to Level 3 Structural Analysis Student Sheets)

3.7 Syllabication: VC/CV

*Divide this word into syllables: **summer**.*
(sum/mer)

		Pre-	Post-
winter	(win/ter)		
basket	(bas/ket)		
better	(bet/ter)		
after	(af/ter)		
ladder	(lad/der)		
signal	(sig/nal)		
Score			

3.9 Syllabication: VC/V

*Divide this word into syllables: **panic**.*
(pan/ic)

		Pre-	Post-
cabin	(cab/in)		
wagon	(wag/on)		
dragon	(drag/on)		
robin	(rob/in)		
lemon	(lem/on)		
melon	(mel/on)		
Score			

3.8 Syllabication: V/CV

*Divide this word into syllables: **robot**.*
(ro/bot)

		Pre-	Post-
hotel	(ho/tel)		
diver	(di/ver)		
tiger	(ti/ger)		
music	(mu/sic)		
bacon	(ba/con)		
paper	(pa/per)		
Score			

Level 3 Informal Assessment of Structural Analysis (continued)

Directions: Mark a + for a correct response and a – for an incorrect response.

Name		Date
Grade	Teacher	
Examiner		

Level 3

First Grade-
Second Grade

Student Assessment
Sheets

Level 3 Print Awareness: Letter Recognition Student Sheet

3.2 Uppercase

M	S	F	P	A	T
K	B	G	I	N	W
D	J	O	L	C	H
U	R	V	E	Q	Y
X	Z				

3.3 Lowercase

m	s	f	p	a	t
k	b	g	i	n	w
d	j	o	l	c	h
u	r	v	e	q	y
x	z				

3.4 Digraphs

shop   this   chalk

whale   fish   lunch

3.5 Blends

block   green   fast

skate   sand   play

Level 3 Synthetic Phonics Student Sheet

3.1 Consonants

m   s   t   d   n

---

f   p   j   h   g

---

b   w   l   r   c

---

k   v   y   q

---

x   z

3.2/3.3 Long and Short Vowels

a   e   i   o   u

Level 3 Synthetic Phonics Student Sheet (continued)

3.4 Consonant Digraphs

sh   ch   th   wh   ph

3.5 Consonant Blends

cl   gr   st   bl   sk

3.6 *R*-Controlled Vowels

ar   er   ir   or   ur

3.7 Vowel Digraphs

ai   ee   oa   oe   ie

3.8 Diphthongs

oy   ow   oi   ou

3.9 Phoneme Segmenting and Blending

Practice item: no

---

me   go   sat   fill   men   nest

3.2 Word Families: Production

Practice item:

hop   top   _____

---

tip   lip   _____

make   bake   _____

sack   pack   _____

bell   tell   _____

dot   hot   _____

bump   jump   _____

Practice item:

sit	**Change *s* to *b***	_____

---

top	**Change *t* to *m***	_____
lip	**Change *l* to *s***	_____
car	**Change *c* to *f***	_____
boat	**Change *b* to *g***	_____
meet	**Change *m* to *b***	_____
look	**Change *l* to *b***	_____
joy	**Change *j* to *t***	_____

Practice item:

| sit | Change *t* to *p* | _____ |

---

lot	Change *t* to *g*	_____
pen	Change *n* to *t*	_____
hip	Change *p* to *d*	_____
shot	Change *t* to *p*	_____
plug	Change *g* to *b*	_____
meet	Change *m* to *k*	_____

Practice item:

sit	**Change _i_ to _a_**	_____

_____

make	**Change _a_ to _i_**	_____
ride	**Change _i_ to _o_**	_____
wade	**Change _a_ to _i_**	_____
mud	**Change _u_ to _a_**	_____
ten	**Change _e_ to _i_**	_____
stop	**Change _o_ to _e_**	_____

Level 3 Vowel Patterns Student Sheet

3.1 Closed

fam	ot
het	nust
ish	stim

3.2 Open

bo	ta
li	ne
mu	vo

3.3 Silent _e_

nake	pere
fute	stide
mive	bose

3.4 Bossy _r_

jart	kird
gorf	murt
derp	harb

3.5 Double Vowel Talkers

tain	**meab**
leep	**boe**
poat	**tay**

3.6 Double Vowel Whiners

mout	**voil**
noy	**bawp**
pown	**goom**

3.7 Consonant + *le*

caple	**rizzle**
durkle	**hottle**
pubble	**tifle**

Practice item:

runs

---

friendly　　　**playful**

turning　　　**buttons**

talking　　　**heated**

Practice item:

airplanes

---

pets   wanted

books   talking

walked   playing

3.3 Affixes: Prefixes

Practice item:
dislike

---

replay   # preview   # unhappy

unable   # rewrite   # disappear

3.4 Compound Words

Practice item:
milkshake

---

sunshine   # outside

doghouse   # fireman

railroad   # blackboard

Practice item:

can not _____

_____

he is _____

let us _____

we will _____

is not _____

I am _____

did not _____

3.6 Syllabication: C + *le*

Practice item:

apple

---

table	purple	cycle
bubble	rifle	puddle

3.7 Syllabication: VC/CV

Practice item:

summer

---

winter	better	ladder
basket	after	signal

3.8 Syllabication: V/CV

Practice item:
robot

---

hotel	**tiger**	**bacon**
diver	**music**	**paper**

3.9 Syllabication: VC/V

Practice item:
panic

---

cabin	**dragon**	**lemon**
wagon	**robin**	**melon**

Level 3

First Grade-
Second Grade

Lesson Plans

Level 3 Prototype Lessons

Level 3 Prototype Lessons

Level 3 Prototype Lessons

Skill   **Page**

Structural analysis

Level 3 Developmental Lessons

The lessons that follow are coded to the previous assessment items. Many different types of children's literature, such as those used for shared reading and guided reading, poems, songs, chants, and stories from home and/or the library are recommended for lessons. For simplicity, however, the following lesson plans are based on only two texts:

The Little Yellow Chicken by Joy Cowley (SUNSHINE™, The Wright Group)

My Wonderful Aunt, Story Five by Margaret Mahy (SUNSHINE™, The Wright Group)

These lesson plans are merely examples; teachers should develop their own lessons for whatever literature is planned for the week. Blackline masters are provided in Appendix 1 for use in developing lesson plans.

Level 3 Lesson Plan Format

Book Title: *The Little Yellow Chicken*		
Process	*Materials*	*Activity*
Preread it	Big Book	Develop schema by discussing book cover and web ideas.
Read it	Big Book	Read the story, pointing to the initial letter of each word.
Reread it	Big Book	Read the story again, inviting students to join in the reading at any time.
Discuss it	Big Book	Talk about the story. Ask open-ended questions.
React to it	Big Books: *The Little Red Hen* and *The Little Yellow Chicken;* Venn diagrams	Compare and contrast *The Little Red Hen* and *The Little Yellow Chicken* using a Venn diagram.
Code it	Following this lesson plan are skill lessons based on this book.	
Apply it	Big Book	Reread the whole story. Observe students for accuracy and fluency.
Transfer it	Big Book: *My Wonderful Aunt, Story Five*	

Level 3 Lesson Plan Format

Book Title: *My Wonderful Aunt, Story Five*		
Process	***Materials***	***Activity***
Preread it	Big Book	Ask students to predict what the lady on the cover is painting. Ask then to explain why. Where is she and what is the cat holding?
Read it	Big Book	Read the story, pointing to the initial letter of each word.
Reread it	Big Book	Read the story again, inviting students to join in the reading at any time.
Discuss it	Big Book	Talk about the story. Ask open-ended questions. Discuss vocabulary: burrow, capers, budgies, and bray.
React to it	Big Book	Have students role-play part of the story.
Code it	Following this lesson plan are skill lessons based on this book.	
Apply it	Big Book	Reread the whole story. Observe students for accuracy and fluency.
Transfer it	New Book	

Coding lesson: phonological awareness
Skill: rhyming word identification
Title: *The Little Yellow Chicken*
Materials: Big Book, drawing materials

Procedures:

1. Remind students that rhyming words have the same sounds at the end, like *sat* and *cat*.

2. Read p. 3, stressing the words *bee* and *me*.

3. Ask students what words rhyme.

4. Brainstorm other words that rhyme with *bee* and *me*.

5. Have students draw pictures for the rhyming words and display them on the word wall.

Transfer:

Using *My Wonderful Aunt, Story Five:*

1. Read several pages and have students listen and identify the rhyming words: aunt, can't; ground, found; stage, age; mail, sale; wall, all; papers, capers.

2. Have students draw pictures for sets of rhyming words.

3. Brainstorm other words that rhyme with the selected words. Have students draw pictures and display them.

3.2 Segmenting: Words in Sentences

Coding lesson: phonological awareness
Skill: segmenting of words in a sentence
Title: *The Little Yellow Chicken*
Materials: Big Book; colored disks

Procedures:

1. Choose sentences to be read orally.

2. As students listen, read a sentence from a selected page.

3. Reread and clap once for each word.

4. Invite students to clap with you.

5. Repeat the process with several other sentences.

Transfer:

Using *My Wonderful Aunt, Story Five:*

1. Have students place six to eight colored disks in rows on their desks.

2. As you read a sentence, have students move a disk for each word they hear.

3. Repeat with other sentences (use sentences with different numbers of words).

3.3/3.6 Segmenting and Blending Compound Words

Coding lesson: phonological awareness
Skill: segmenting and blending of compound words
Title: *The Little Yellow Chicken*
Materials: Big Book, pictures of compound words, scissors, drawing materials

Procedures:

1. Choose a compound word from the story such as *grandmother*.

2. Copy (or draw) a picture of the little red hen and ask students to say the big word *grandmother* with you, listening for the two small words in it (*grand* and *mother*).

3. As students say each small word, cut the picture into two pieces and then have students put the word together, saying *grandmother*.

4. Repeat with other compound words, such as *everything* and *himself*.

Transfer:

Using *My Wonderful Aunt, Story Five:*

1. Repeat the activity with words from the story: *neighborhood* and *teapot*.

2. Have students draw pictures to depict each compound word.

3. Have students cut each picture and practice "breaking" and "making" each compound word, as they say the two small parts and the one big word.

3.4/3.7 Segmenting and Blending Syllables

Coding lesson: phonological awareness
Skill: segmenting and blending of syllables
Title: *The Little Yellow Chicken*
Materials: Big Book; colored blocks

Procedures:

1. Remind students how to "feel" syllables or chunks of words (place your hand under your chin and feel how each time you say a word part (chunk or syllable), your jaw drops).

2. Practice with each child to say and feel the parts in their names.

3. Choose two- and three-syllable words from the story, such as *yellow, little, beetle, table, delicious, fantastic,* and *amazing.*

4. Ask students to feel their jaw move for each word part and to count the parts with their other hand, using one finger for each syllable.

5. Have students feel the word break into its parts. Then have them make the whole word again: Fan – tas – tic (segment). Fantastic (blend).

Transfer:

Using *My Wonderful Aunt, Story Five:*

1. Repeat the activity with two-, three-, and four- syllable words (*burrow, wonderful, delivering*).

2. Have students say a word, count the number of syllables within the word, and place that number of blocks in a row.

3. Have students move a block for each syllable they hear (segment).

4. Have students push blocks together as they say the whole word (blend).

3.5/3.8 Segmenting and Blending Phonemes

Coding lesson: phonological awareness
Skill: segmenting and blending of phonemes
Title: *The Little Yellow Chicken*
Materials: Big Book; picture cards; scissors; pocket chart; colored disks or connecting blocks

Procedures:

1. Choose words from the story with two or three phonemes (*bee, hen, red, food*).

2. Show students how to cut a piece of a picture card for each sound. Say *hen.* Say /*h*/ and cut a third of the picture. Say /*e*/ and cut another third. Say /*n*/ and show the last third of the picture.

3. As you cut each piece, place it in the pocket chart.

4. After all the parts are in the chart, say the whole word together: *hen.*

5. Have students cut other pictures as they segment a word.

6. Be sure to say the whole word together (blend) when finished.

Transfer:

Using *My Wonderful Aunt, Story Five:*

1. Repeat the activity with words from the story: *aunt, bath, dog, clown.*

2. Have students move colored disks or connecting blocks for each sound (not each letter).

3. Have students push disks together or connect blocks as they say a whole word (blending).

Coding lesson: phonological awareness
Skill: identification of initial phonemes
Title: *The Little Yellow Chicken*
Materials: Big Book; chart paper for pictures; collage materials

Procedures:

1. Choose words from the story that begin with /b/: *buzz, big, bee, brown, beetle, bugging, by, backs.*

2. Say the selected words aloud, stressing the initial sound, as students listen.

3. Discuss what your lips do when you make the /b/ sound, as students observe the position of your mouth and lips.

4. Repeat /b/ words with the students, as they feel their own mouths and lips.

5. Make a chart of pictures (draw them or cut them from magazines) that begin with /b/. Display them on the word wall.

Transfer:

Using *My Wonderful Aunt, Story Five:*

1. Repeat the activity with words from the story that begin with /w/: *wonderful, wouldn't, when, wanted, were, we, work, went, wall, will, with, wink.*

2. Reread the story and have students raise their hands every time they hear a word that begins with the /w/ sound.

3. Made a collage of pictures beginning with /w/ and display it.

3.10 Phoneme Identification: Final

Coding lesson: phonological awareness
Skill: identification of final phonemes
Title: *The Little Yellow Chicken*
Materials: Big Book; chart paper; colored markers, collage materials

Procedures:

1. Choose words from the story that end with /p/: *help, hop, stop.*

2. Read selected words aloud, stressing the final /p/ sound, as students listen.

3. Discuss what your lips do when you make the /p/ sound, as students observe the position of your mouth and lips.

4. Repeat words that end in /p/ with students as they feel their own mouths and lips.

5. Made a chart of pictures (draw them or cut them out of magazines) that end with /p/. Display them on the word wall.

Transfer:

Using *My Wonderful Aunt, Story Five:*

1. Repeat the activity with words from the story that end in /l/: *wonderful, mail, sale, wall.*

2. Reread the story and have students stand every time they hear a word that ends with /l/.

3. Brainstorm and make a collage of final /l/ pictures. Display the pictures.

3.11 Phoneme Identification: Medial

Coding lesson: phonological awareness
Skill: identification of medial phonemes
Title: *The Little Yellow Chicken*
Materials: Big Book; chart paper; drawing or collage materials

Procedures:

1. Choose words for the story that contain a medial /e/ sound: *red, hen, set, let, them, then.*

2. Read the selected words aloud stressing the medial /e/ sound as students listen.

3. Discuss what your lips do when you make the /e/ sound, as students observe the position of your mouth and lips. Remind students of sign language clues.

4. Repeat medial /e/ words with the students as they feel their own mouths and lips. They may also remember the "Ed the elephant" vowel association.

5. Made a chart of pictures (draw them or cut them out of magazines) that contain a medial /e/. Display them on the word wall.

Transfer:

Using *My Wonderful Aunt, Story Five:*

1. Repeat the activity with words from the story that contain the medial /a/ sound: *came, mail, sale, take, wail, fair, gave.*

2. Reread the story and have the students clap every time they hear a word that contains the medial /a/.

3. Brainstorm and make a collage of medial /a/ pictures. Display them.

3.12 Manipulation: Deletion

Coding lesson: phonological awareness
Skill: deleting parts of words
Title: *The Little Yellow Chicken*
Materials: Big Book; colored blocks

Procedures:

1. Choose a compound word from the story such as *grandmother.*

2. Have students place two colored blocks on their desks to represent the two parts of *grandmother.* Have them touch each block as they say *grandmother.*

3. Ask students to say *grandmother* again but without *grand.* As they do this, have them remove the first block.

4. Repeat with *everything.* Say *everything.* Say it again but don't say *thing.* As students remove the second block, have them say *every.*

5. Gradually repeat with syllables (*yel-low*), and eventually phonemes (*m-e*), deleting the first or second syllable or phoneme.

Transfer:

Using *My Wonderful Aunt, Story Five:*

1. Repeat the activity with compound words from the story: *neighborhood, teapot.*

2. As students become proficient, have them use multisyllabic words. Say *sensation.* Have students place three blocks on their desks. Say it again but don't say *sen.* Have students remove the first block and say *sation.* Later, use words with several sounds such as *ground* (five blocks). Say it again but don't say /g/ (*round*).

3.13 Manipulation: Substitution: Initial Sounds

Coding lesson: phonological awareness
Skill: substituting initial sounds
Title: *The Little Yellow Chicken*
Materials: Big Book; colored blocks or chips (four different colors)

Procedures:

1. Choose a word from the story such as *set*. Say the word slowly so students can hear each phoneme (/s/ /e/ /t/).

2. Have students represent each phoneme with a block or chip:
   /s/= green block /e/= yellow block /t/= red block

3. Ask students to change *set* to *met*.

4. Have students change the green block to another color (blue), demonstrating that the first sound /s/ has changed to /m/.

5. Repeat with other words from the story. Change *bee* to *see* and *time* to *lime*.

Transfer:

Using *My Wonderful Aunt, Story Five:*

1. Repeat the activity with words from the story: change *found* to *round* and *clock* to *block*.

2. Have students say *found*. Ask them to change the /f/ to /r/ and say the new word (*round*).

3. Brainstorm other words that can be made by changing the initial sound. Nonsense words are acceptable.

3.14 Manipulation: Substitution: Final Sounds

Coding lesson: phonological awareness
Skill: substituting final sounds
Title: *The Little Yellow Chicken*
Materials: Big Book; colored blocks or chips (four different colors)

Procedures:

1. Choose a word from the story such as *hop*. Say the word slowly so students can hear each phoneme (/h/ /o/ /p/).

2. Have students represent each phoneme with a block or chip:
   /h/= green block /o/= yellow block /p/= red block

3. Ask students to change *hop* to *hot*.

4. Have students change the red block to another color (blue), demonstrating that the last sound /p/ has changed to /t/.

5. Repeat with other words from the story. Change *but* to *bug* and *hen* to *head*.

Transfer:

Using *My Wonderful Aunt, Story Five:*

1. Repeat the activity with words from the story: change *crown* to *crowd* and *bath* to *bag*.

2. Have students say *crown*. Ask them to change the /n/ to /d/ and say the new word (*crowd*).

3. Brainstorm other words that can be made by changing the final sound. Nonsense words are acceptable.

3.15 Manipulation: Substitution: Medial Sounds

Coding lesson: phonological awareness

Skill: substituting medial sounds

Title: *The Little Yellow Chicken*

Materials: Big Book; colored blocks or chips (four different colors)

Procedures:

1. Choose a word from the story such as *big*. Say the word slowly so students can hear each phoneme (/b/ /i/ /g/).

2. Have students represent each phoneme with a block or chip:
   /b/ = green block /i/ = yellow block /g/ = red block

3. Ask students to change *big* to *bag*.

4. Have students change the yellow block to another color (blue), demonstrating that the middle sound /i/ has changed to /a/.

5. Repeat with other words from the story. Change *hop* to *hip* and *time* to *team.*

Transfer:

Using *My Wonderful Aunt, Story Five:*

1. Repeat the activity with words from the story: change *clown* to *clean* and *cream* to *crime.*

2. Have students say *clown*. Ask them to change the /ow/ to /ee/ and say the new word (*clean*).

3. Brainstorm other words that can be made by changing the medial (middle) sound. Nonsense words are acceptable.

3.1 Concepts of Print

Coding lesson: print awareness
Skill: concepts of print familiarity
Title: *The Little Yellow Chicken*
Materials: Big Book

Procedures:

During the "skill" segment of the lesson ask students to

- show you where to start reading
- show you the direction (left to right)
- show you a "return sweep"
- show you page sequence
- show you "words and spaces"
- show you top and bottom
- show you words versus letters

Transfer:

Have children repeat the skills with other books, posters, reproductions and innovations around the room.

Coding lesson: print awareness
Skill: recognition of uppercase letters
Title: *The Little Yellow Chicken*
Materials: Big Book; wax-covered yarn or colored transparent tape; magnifying glass

Procedures:

1. Select a page from the story that contains a target letter such as *H* (pp. 2-3).

2. Reread pages 2 and 3.

3. Write the uppercase letter *H* on the board and review its shape and form (a ladder with just one step).

4. Ask students to locate in the Big Book an uppercase *H* on pp. 2–3 (*He, His, Hop)* and frame the *H* with wax-covered yarn or a piece of colored transparent tape.

5. Repeat with other target uppercase letters.

Transfer:

Using *My Wonderful Aunt, Story Five:*

1. Repeat the activity with words from *My Wonderful Aunt,* using various uppercase letters: *S* on p. 6: *Sale, She, Saying.*

2. Use a magnifying glass and say *I spy an uppercase* **S**. Have students pretend to be letter detectives and find the target letter on the selected page with the magnifying glass.

Coding lesson: print awareness
Skill: recognition of lowercase letters
Title: *The Little Yellow Chicken*
Materials: Big Book; wax-covered yarn or colored transparent tape; magnifying glass; overhead projector

Procedures:

1. Select a page from the story that contains a target letter: *b* (p. 3).

2. Reread page 3.

3. Write the lowercase letter *b* on the board (trace over the stick in green) and review its name, shape, and form (a bat and a ball and the bat comes first!).

4. Ask students to locate in the Big Book a lowercase *b* on p. 3 (*bee, big, brown, beetle, bugging, by*) and frame it with wax-covered yarn or a piece of colored transparent tape.

5. Repeat with other target lowercase letters.

Transfer:

Using *My Wonderful Aunt, Story Five:*

1. Repeat the activity with the letter *p* on page 12: *happy, shoppers, popcorn, peanuts.*

2. Use a magnifying glass and say *I spy a lowercase p.* Have students pretend to be letter detectives and find the target letter on the selected page with the magnifying glass.

3. Have students trace over the selected letters on a blank transparency.

Coding lesson: print awareness

Skill: recognition of blends

Title: *The Little Yellow Chicken*

Materials: Big Book; wax-covered yarn or colored transparent tape; chart paper and pen; magnifying glass; overhead projector

Procedures:

1. Select a target blend such as *fr* (*friends, frog*) on pp. 2-3.

2. Reread pages 2-3.

3. Write the *fr* blend on the board and review the letters' names, shapes, and forms. Remind students that blends slide their sounds together.

4. Ask students to locate in the Big Book the *fr* blends. Have them highlight them with wax-covered yarn or a piece of colored transparent tape.

5. Have students brainstorm other words that begin with *fr.* Write the words on a chart, highlighting all the *fr* blends in green.

Transfer:

Using *My Wonderful Aunt, Story Five:*

1. Repeat the activity with *br* (*broadly, bray, bring*) on p. 16.

2. Use a magnifying glass and say *I spy a br blend.* Have students pretend to be letter detectives and find the target blend on the selected page with the magnifying glass.

3. Have students trace over the selected blends on a blank transparency.

Coding lesson: print awareness

Skill: recognition of digraphs

Title: *The Little Yellow Chicken*

Materials: Big Book; wax-covered yarn; colored highlighting tape; highlighters; magnifying glass; overhead projector

Procedures:

1. Select a target digraph such as *ch* in *chicken.*

2. Reread the story.

3. Write the *ch* digraph on the board and review the letters' names, shapes, and forms. Tell students **ch** *makes the sound /ch/ like when we sneeze and say* **ah-ah-choo**. *It's the loud one (/sh/ is the quiet one)!*

4. Ask students to locate in the Big Book all the *ch* digraphs. Ask them to highlight them with wax-covered yarn or highlighting tape. See how many they can find (fourteen).

5. Have students brainstorm other words that begin (or end) with *ch.* Write the words on a chart, highlighting all the *ch* digraphs in blue.

Transfer:

Using *My Wonderful Aunt, Story Five:*

1. Repeat the activity with *sh* (*she, shoppers*).

2. Use a magnifying glass and say *I spy an* **sh** *digraph.* Have students pretend to be letter detectives and find the target digraph on the selected pages with the magnifying glass.

3. Have students trace over the selected digraphs on a blank transparency.

3.1 Consonants

Coding lesson: synthetic phonics

Skill: consonants: sound-symbol association

Title: *The Little Yellow Chicken*

Materials: Big Book; picture charts from phonological awareness plans; wax-covered yarn or colored transparent tape

Procedures: These procedures may be used with any consonant and any book.

1. If teaching the letter *b*, using words from *The Little Yellow Chicken*, refer to phonological awareness lesson plan 3.9.

2. Reread the story and have students clap each time they hear a word beginning like *bee: buzz, big, brown, beetle, bugging, by, backs*.

3. Write the letter *b* on the board (review print awareness lesson plan 3.3.)

4. Review the /b/ words from the picture chart; write a word under each picture.

5. Have students locate several /b/ words in the Big Book, highlighting them with wax-covered yarn or colored transparent tape.

Transfer: Using *My Wonderful Aunt, Story Five:*

1. Repeat the activity with words from the story that begin with *w*. (See phonological awareness lesson plan 3.9.)

2. Have students practice the correct letter formation of any target consonant with manipulatives at a writing center.

3. Puzzles (teacher-made or purchased) that match consonants and pictures beginning with the selected sound and letter may be used as center activities.

3.2 Long Vowels

Coding lesson: synthetic phonics
Skill: long vowels: sound-symbol association
Title: *The Little Yellow Chicken*
Materials: Big Book; alphabet book or cards

Procedures:

These procedures may be used with any long vowel and any book.

1. Remind students that the important vowels are *a, e, i, o,* and *u* and that, when we say (or sing) the alphabet, the vowels say their real names (long vowels).

2. Ask students to listen as you read page 3 from *The Little Yellow Chicken.*

3. Repeat the words *bee* and *me,* stressing the long *e* sound.

4. Write the letter *e* on the board. Show students the letters in an alphabet book or card. Have them say its name.

5. Read on and have students clap when they hear other words with the long *e* sound (*eat, tea, he, we, beetle*).

6. Repeat with other long vowel sounds from the story: *i* (*by, time, I'm*) and *o* (*so, opened*). Then have students brainstorm more long vowel words.

Transfer: Using *My Wonderful Aunt, Story Five,* repeat the activity with words from the story:

    a (say, came, stage, age, mail, sale, papers, take, day)

    e (she, be, we, trees, needs, eagerly, peanuts, queen, cream)

    i (I, hide, my, like, buy, ice, smile)

    o (posters, go, so)

    u (blue, music)

Coding lesson: synthetic phonics

Skill: short vowels: sound-symbol association

Title: *The Little Yellow Chicken*

Materials: Big Book; alphabet book or cards

Procedures:

These procedures may be used with any short vowel and any book.

1. Remind students that the important vowels are *a, e, i, o,* and *u* and that when we say (or sing) the alphabet, the vowels say their real names (long vowels). But sometimes they say their *special sounds* (short vowel sounds). Review associative objects and pictures.

2. Ask students to listen as you read page 3 from *The Little Yellow Chicken.*

3. Repeat the words *hop, frog, stop,* and *shopping,* stressing the short *o* sound (as in *octopus).*

4. Write the letter *o* on the board. Show the letter *o* book or card. Have students say its special sound.

5. Read on and have students clap when they hear these words repeated.

6. Gradually repeat with other short vowel words from the story: *a (at, backs), e (help, set, red, hen, let), i (will, his, big, did).* Then have students brainstorm more short vowel words.

Transfer: Using *My Wonderful Aunt, Story Five,* repeat the activity with words from the story:

short a (an, bath, ad, had, band, cat, hat, at), short e (went, them, let, tents, well); short i (in, rid, lid, with, pick, bit); short o (on, lost, hop, hot, dog, box, clocks, not), short u (dug, but, up, drums).

Coding lesson: synthetic phonics
Skill: consonant digraphs: sound-symbol association
Title: *The Little Yellow Chicken*
Materials: Big Book; wax-covered yarn or colored transparent tape

Procedures:

These procedures may be used with any consonant digraph and any book.

1. Introduce digraphs as *two letters that make one very different sound: /sh/ is the quiet one (Sh! The baby's sleeping!); /ch/ is the LOUD one (ah, ah, ah, CHOO!); /th/ is the only time you can stick your tongue out at me!* As you write each digraph on the board in blue, write one line under the two letters to indicate one sound.

2. Ask students to listen as you read from *The Little Yellow Chicken.*

3. Repeat the words *chicken, shopping, shook, the, them, thought, then, that's,* and *grandmother,* stressing the */ch/, /sh/,* and */th/* digraphs.

4. Reread and have students clap when they hear these words repeated.

5. Have students locate words with digraphs in the Big Book. Ask them to highlight them with wax-covered yarn or colored transparent tape.

6. Have students brainstorm other words with consonant digraphs in both the initial and final positions.

Transfer: Using *My Wonderful Aunt, Story Five:*

1. Repeat the activity with words from the story: *sh (she, shoppers)* and *th (there, the, that, bath, them, grandfather, then, they, something).*

2. Make a chart for the word wall with various digraphs.

3. Have students construct simple words with */sh/, /ch/, /th/.*

3.5 Consonant Blends

<table>
<tr><td colspan="2">

Coding lesson: synthetic phonics
</td></tr>
<tr><td colspan="2">

Skill: consonant blends: sound-symbol association
</td></tr>
<tr><td colspan="2">

Title: *The Little Yellow Chicken*
</td></tr>
<tr><td colspan="2">

Materials: Big Book; wax-covered yarn; alphabet book or cards; drawing materials
</td></tr>
<tr><td colspan="2">

Procedures:

These procedures may be used with any consonant blend and any book.

1. Introduce blends as *two or three sounds next to each other.* As you write a blend from the story on the board in green, make a curved line under the two or three letters to indicate that the sounds slide together.

2. Ask students to listen as you read from *The Little Yellow Chicken.*

3. Repeat the words *friends, brown, stop, smelled,* and *starving,* stressing the *fr, br, sm,* and *st* blends, and showing the book or card with the corresponding blend.

4. Reread and have students clap when they hear these words repeated.

5. Have students locate words with blends in the Big Book and highlight them with wax-covered yarn or transparent tape.

6. Have students brainstorm other words with consonant blends, make up and illustrate alliterative sentences (e.g., *Fred's friends ate french fries on Friday.*) Write blends on a chart for the word wall.
</td></tr>
<tr><td colspan="2">

Transfer: Using *My Wonderful Aunt, Story Five,* repeat with words from the story: *cl (clown), bl (blue), dr (drum), br (bring, brought, bray), cr (crumbs, crowd, crown), gr (great, grumbled, grandfather, ground), tr (trumpets), st (stood),* and *sm (smell, smiled).*
</td></tr>
</table>

3.6 R-Controlled Vowels

Coding lesson: synthetic phonics

Skill: *r*-controlled vowels: sound-symbol association

Title: *The Little Yellow Chicken*

Materials: Big Book; wax-covered yarn or colored transparent tape; drawing materials

---

Procedures:

These procedures may be used with any *r*-controlled word and any book.

1. Introduce *r*-controlled or bossy *r* words as *words that have a vowel followed by the letter* **r**. See the Vowel Patterns lesson plan 3.4. *Because the* **r** *is so bossy (or takes control), it tells the vowel to say its sound:* /**ar**/, /**or**/, /**er**/, /**ir**/, /**ur**/. *The vowel can't say its real name (long) or its special sound (short).*

2. Ask students to listen as you read from *The Little Yellow Chicken*.

3. Repeat the words *for, party,* and *turned,* stressing the *or, ar,* and *ur* patterns.

4. Reread and have students clap when they hear these words repeated.

5. Have students locate words with blends in the Big Book and highlight them with wax-covered yarn or transparent tape.

6. Have students brainstorm other *r*-controlled words. List them on a chart for the word wall.

Transfer:

Using *My Wonderful Aunt, Story Five*:

1. Repeat the activity with words from the story (*her, bird, corn, scorn, sport*).

2. Ask students to brainstorm other *r*-controlled words and illustrate them.

Coding lesson: synthetic phonics
Skill: vowel digraphs: sound-symbol association
Title: *The Little Yellow Chicken*
Materials: Big Book; wax-covered yarn or colored transparent tape; wall charts, drawing materials

Procedures: These procedures may be used with any vowel digraph and any book.

1. Introduce the concept of double vowel talkers (see Vowel Patterns lesson plan 3.5). *When two vowels go walking, the first one does the talking and says its name.*

2. Ask students to listen as you read from *The Little Yellow Chicken.*

3. On the board, write the words *bee, tea,* and *eat,* stressing the *ee* and *ea* patterns. Make sure the vowels are written in red.

4. Say the words with the students, asking them to tell you what vowel's name they hear (*e*).

5. Have students locate words with vowel digraphs in the Big Book or in other print around the room. Highlight them with wax-covered yarn or colored transparent tape.

6. Have students brainstorm other words with vowel digraphs. List them on a chart for the word wall.

Transfer: Using *My Wonderful Aunt, Story Five:*

1. Repeat the activity with words from the story (*mail, day, trees, needs, bray*).

2. Have students locate other vowel digraph (or double vowel talker) words in the story and verbalize their reasons for their selections.

3. Ask students to brainstorm other vowel digraph words and illustrate them.

Coding lesson: synthetic phonics

Skill: vowel diphthongs: sound-symbol association

Title: *The Little Yellow Chicken*

Materials: Big Book; magnetic letters, alphabet chips; wax-covered yarn or colored transparent tape; wall charts, drawing materials

Procedures:

These procedures may be used with any vowel diphthong and any book.

1. Introduce the concept of double vowel whiners (see Vowel Patterns lesson plan 3.6). *Sometimes, when two vowels are next to each other, they whine a funny sound, like /ow/, /oy/, /oo/.*

2. Ask students to listen as you read from *The Little Yellow Chicken.*

3. On the board, write the word *brown,* stressing the *ow* pattern—make sure the vowels are written in red (including the *w*).

4. Have a student come to the board to frame the *ow.*

5. Have students locate words with vowel diphthongs in the Big Book (*now, food, good, shook*) or in other print around the room and highlight the dipthongs with wax-covered yarn or colored transparent tape.

6. Have students construct words with alphabet chips, noticing the two adjacent red chips. List the words on a chart for the word wall.

Transfer: Using *My Wonderful Aunt, Story Five:*

1. Repeat the activity with words from the story (*ground, clown, crown, took, round, found, frown, mew, saw*).

2. Have students locate vowel diphthongs (or double vowel whiners) in words in the story and verbalize the reasons for their selections.

3. Ask students to brainstorm other vowel diphthong words and illustrate them.

Coding lesson: synthetic phonics
Skill: blending of phonemes
Title: *The Little Yellow Chicken*
Materials: Big Book; magnetic board and letters; sticky notes; alphabet tiles or chips

Procedures:

1. Select several one-syllable words from the story such as *hop, big,* and *frog.*

2. Have students construct each word with magnetic letters, saying each sound as it is added; then have them say the whole word.

3. Write words on sticky notes and have students find the words in the book.

Transfer:

Using *My Wonderful Aunt, Story Five:*

1. Repeat the activity with words from the story (*dug, lid, bath, band*).

2. Have students use a variety of alphabet tiles or chips (vowels may be coded in red) to create the words.

3. Play a hangman game, using dashes for letters. Have students guess the letters they hear in a word and then say the word.

3.2 Word Families: Production

Coding lesson: analytic phonics
Skill: production of word families
Title: *The Little Yellow Chicken*
Materials: Big Book; magnetic letters, alphabet chips; wax-covered yarn or colored transparent tape; drawing materials; reproductions or wall charts

Procedures:

These procedures may be used with any word family and any book.

1. Introduce the concept of a word family. *Just like we all have a family name, words have families too. In* **The Little Yellow Chicken***, the words* **hop** *and* **stop** *belong to the* **op** *family.*

2. On the board, write the words *hop* and *stop* (make sure the *op* is written in red). Ask students what is the same in these words (*op*).

3. Have a student come to the board to trace over or underline the *op* rime.

4. Have students brainstorm other *op* words (real or nonsense) and list them on a chart for the word wall. Repeat with the *ig* family (*big*) and the *ed* family (*red*).

5. Have students locate other *op, ig,* and *ed* words around the room and highlight them with wax-covered yarn or colored transparent tape.

Transfer: Using *My Wonderful Aunt, Story Five:*

1. Repeat the activity with other words from the story: *say, rid, hot, cat, like,* and *round.*

2. Have students locate these word families embedded in text, framing each with wax-covered yarn or colored transparent tape.

3. Ask students to brainstorm other words in these word families and illustrate them.

3.3 Word Families: Substitution of Initial Letter

Coding lesson: analytic phonics
Skill: substitution of an initial letter
Title: *The Little Yellow Chicken*
Materials: Big Book; colored blocks; alphabet chips or tiles; write-on boards and markers; wall charts

Procedures:

1. Review the concept of a word family and select one word family from a previous lesson, such as *op*.

2. Write the word *hop* on the board; erase the *h*, and write a *t* in its place. Read the new word, *top*.

3. Have a student come to the board to change the *t* to *m*; ask students what the new word is (*mop*). Ask for another volunteer to change the *m* to *p* (*pop*). Use colored blocks to make the words. Have students listen to the sounds and then replace the letters that change.

4. Have students construct these words with alphabet chips or tiles at their desks, substituting initial consonants or blends.

5. Repeat with other word families such as *ig* and *ed*.

Transfer: Using *My Wonderful Aunt, Story Five:*

1. Repeat the activity with words from the story: *say, rid, hot, cat, like,* and *round.*

2. Repeat the above activity with write-on boards and colored markers. Use green marker for initial consonant substitutions and red for word families.

3. Make a list of word families and post them on the word wall.

3.4 Word Families: Substitution of Final Letter

Coding lesson: analytic phonics
Skill: substitution of the final letter
Title: *The Little Yellow Chicken*
Materials: Big Book; colored blocks; alphabet chips or tiles; write-on boards and markers

Procedures:

1. Review the concept of a word family and select one word family from a previous lesson, such as *op*.

2. Write the word *hop* on the board; erase the *p* and write a *t* in its place, telling students the new word, *hot*.

3. Have a student come to the board to change the *t* to *g*. Ask students what the new word is (*hog*). Use colored blocks to make the words. Have students listen to the sounds and then replace the letters that change.

4. Have students construct these words with alphabet chips or tiles at their desks, substituting final consonants. See how many different words can be made by substituting the final consonant; nonsense words are acceptable.

5. Repeat with other word families such as *big* (bit, bib, bid) and *him* (hid, hip, hit).

Transfer:

Using *My Wonderful Aunt, Story Five*:

1. Repeat the activity with words from the story: *rid, hot, cat,* and *bath*.

2. Repeat the activity with write-on boards and colored markers. Use green marker for the initial consonant, red for the vowel, and blue for the final consonant substitutions.

3.5 Word Families: Substitution of Medial Letter

Coding lesson: analytic phonics
Skill: substitution of a middle letter
Title: *The Little Yellow Chicken*
Materials: Big Book; alphabet chips or tiles; write-on boards and markers

Procedures:

1. Review the concept of a word family and select one word family from a previous lesson such as *ig*.

2. Write the word *big* on the board; erase the *i* and write an *a* in its place, telling students the new word, *bag*.

3. Have a student come to the board to change the *a* to *u*. Ask students what the new word is (*bug*). Use colored blocks to make the words. Have students listen to the sounds and then place the letters.

4. Have students construct these words with alphabet chips or tiles at their desks, substituting medial vowels. See how many different words can be made by substituting the middle vowel; nonsense words are acceptable.

5. Repeat with other words such as *hop* (hip, hup) and *him* (ham, hem, hum).

Transfer:

Using *My Wonderful Aunt, Story Five:*

1. Repeat the activity with other words from the story: *rid, hot, cat,* and *dog*.

2. Repeat the activity with write-on boards and colored markers. Use green marker for the initial consonant, red for the vowel substitutions, and blue for the final consonant.

3.1 Vowel Patterns: Closed

Coding lesson: vowel patterns

Skill: identification of the closed vowel pattern

Title: *The Little Yellow Chicken*

Materials: Big Book; color-coded alphabet chips; Vowel Pattern Chart

Procedures:

1. Select a closed vowel pattern word from the story such as *hen*.

2. Write *hen* on the board, coding the *e* in red. (All vowels will be highlighted in red for all vowel patterns.)

3. Explain the concept of a closed vowel pattern: *Like the meat in a sandwich, the vowel is squished in and can only say its special (short) vowel sound.* (/*e*/ as in *Ed the elephant*—review the sign language association).

4. Demonstrate with other closed words: *hop, big, red.*

5. Have students construct words with alphabet chips and notice the one red letter (vowel) closed in by two other letters (consonants).

6. Have students write the words in the closed box of the Vowel Pattern Chart and read the words aloud.

Transfer:

Using *My Wonderful Aunt, Story Five:*

1. Repeat the activity with words from the story: *dug, rid, wigs, bath,* and *drums.*

2. Have students locate other closed vowel pattern words in the story and verbalize the reasons for their selections.

3. Ask students to brainstorm other closed vowel pattern words that rhyme with the selected words.

Coding lesson: vowel patterns
Skill: identification of the open vowel pattern
Title: *The Little Yellow Chicken*
Materials: Big Book; color-coded alphabet chips; Vowel Pattern Chart

Procedures:

1. Select an open vowel pattern word from the story, such as *me.*

2. Write *me* on the board, coding the *e* in red. (All vowels will be highlighted in red for all vowel patterns.)

3. Explain the concept of an open vowel pattern: *Like the meat on an open sandwich, the vowel is on top (at the end) and is free to say its real name (long vowel sound).* See the jingle on lesson plan 2.2.

4. Demonstrate with other open vowel words: *so, by, we.*

5. Have students construct words with color-coded alphabet chips and notice the one red letter (vowel) at the end of the word.

6. Have students write the words in the open box of the Vowel Pattern Chart and read the words aloud.

Transfer:

Using *My Wonderful Aunt, Story Five:*

1. Repeat the activity with words from the story: *my, she, no, be,* and *we.*

2. Have students locate other open vowel pattern words in the story and verbalize the reasons for their selections.

3. Ask students to brainstorm other open vowel pattern words that rhyme with the selected words.

Coding lesson: vowel patterns
Skill: identification of the silent *e* vowel pattern
Title: *The Little Yellow Chicken*
Materials: Big Book; color-coded alphabet chips; Vowel Pattern Chart

Procedures:

1. Select a silent *e* vowel pattern word from the story, such as *time.*

2. Write *time* on the board, coding the *i* and *e* in red. (All vowels will be highlighted in red for all vowel patterns.)

3. Explain the concept of a silent *e* vowel pattern: See lesson plan 2.3. *When a word ends in e, it gives all its power to the other vowel, and that vowel says its real name (long vowel sound).*

4. Demonstrate with other silent *e* words such as *phone.*

5. Have students construct words with color-coded alphabet chips and notice the two red chips (the silent *e* and the other vowel).

6. Have students write the words in the silent *e* box of the Vowel Pattern Chart and read the words aloud.

Transfer:

Using *My Wonderful Aunt, Story Five:*

1. Repeat the activity with words from the story: *hide, came, stage, sale, home,* and *smile.*

2. Have students locate other silent *e* vowel pattern words in the story and verbalize the reasons for their selections.

3. Ask students to brainstorm other silent *e* vowel pattern words that rhyme with the selected words.

3.4 Vowel Patterns: Bossy r

Coding lesson: vowel patterns
Skill: identification of the bossy *r* vowel pattern
Title: *The Little Yellow Chicken*
Materials: Big Book; color-coded alphabet chips; Vowel Pattern Chart

Procedures:

1. Select a bossy *r* vowel pattern word from the story such as *turn.*

2. Write *turn* on the board, coding the *u* in red. (All vowels will be highlighted in red for all vowel patterns.)

3. Explain the concept of a bossy *r* vowel pattern: *When a word has one vowel and the letter r after it, the r is SO bossy, it changes the sound of the vowel (not long or short).* (See lesson plan 2.4.)

4. Demonstrate with other bossy *r* words such as *for.*

5. Have students construct words with color-coded alphabet chips and notice that the red chip (the vowel) is followed by an *r.*

6. Have students place the magnetic word cards (or write words) in the bossy *r* box of the Vowel Pattern Chart and read the words aloud.

Transfer: Using *My Wonderful Aunt, Story Five:*

1. Repeat the activity with words from the story: *her, bird, corn, scorn,* and *sport.*

2. Have students locate other bossy *r* vowel pattern words in the story and verbalize the reasons for their selections.

3. Ask students to brainstorm other bossy *r* vowel pattern words that rhyme with the selected words.

239

3.5 Vowel Patterns: Double Vowel Talkers

Coding lesson: vowel patterns
Skill: identification of the double vowel talker vowel pattern
Title: *The Little Yellow Chicken*
Materials: Big Book; color-coded alphabet chips; Vowel Pattern Chart

Procedures:

1. Select a double vowel talker vowel pattern word from the story such as *tea*.

2. Write *tea* on the board, coding the *ea* in red. (All vowels will be highlighted in red for all vowel patterns.)

3. Explain the concept of a double vowel talker vowel pattern: *When two vowels go walking, the first one does the talking and says its name.* (See lesson plan 2.5.)

4. Demonstrate with other double vowel talker words such as *bee* and *eat*.

5. Have students construct words with color-coded alphabet chips and notice the two red chips next to each other (the first one says its name, the second one is quiet).

6. Have students place the magnetic word cards (or write words) in the double vowel talker box of the Vowel Pattern Chart and read the words aloud.

Transfer:

Using *My Wonderful Aunt, Story Five:*

1. Repeat the activity with words from the story: *mail, trees, day, needs.*

2. Have students locate other double vowel talker vowel pattern words in the story and verbalize the reasons for their selections.

3. Ask students to brainstorm other double vowel talker vowel pattern words that rhyme with the selected words.

3.6 Vowel Patterns: Double Vowel Whiners

Coding lesson: vowel patterns
Skill: identification of the double vowel whiner vowel pattern
Title: *The Little Yellow Chicken*
Materials: Big Book; color-coded alphabet chips; Vowel Pattern Chart

Procedures:

1. Select a double vowel whiner vowel pattern word from the story such as *brown.*

2. Write *brown* on the board, coding the *ow* in red. *W* works like a vowel in *ow* combinations.

3. Explain the concept of a double vowel whiner vowel pattern: *Sometimes when two vowels are together, they whine their sound.* (See lesson plan 2.6.)

4. Demonstrate with other double vowel whiner vowel pattern words such as *food, now, good,* and *shook.*

5. Have students construct words with color-coded alphabet chips and notice the two adjacent red chips.

6. Have students place the magnetic word cards (or write words) in the double vowel whiner box of the Vowel Pattern Chart and read the words aloud.

Transfer:

Using *My Wonderful Aunt, Story Five:*

1. Repeat the activity with words from the story: *ground, clown, took, crown.*

2. Have students locate other double vowel whiner vowel pattern words in the story and verbalize the reasons for their selections.

3. Ask students to brainstorm other double vowel whiner vowel pattern words that rhyme with the selected words.

Coding lesson: vowel patterns

Skill: identification of the consonant + *le* vowel pattern

Title: *The Little Yellow Chicken*

Materials: Big Book; color-coded alphabet chips; Vowel Pattern Chart

Procedures:

1. Select a consonant + *le* vowel pattern word from the story such as *beetle*.

2. Write *beetle* on the board, coding the *le* in red.

3. Explain the concept of a C + *le* vowel pattern: *When a word ends in **le** and there's a consonant before it, we cut the word in half before that consonant:* **bee - tle**.

4. Demonstrate with other C + *le* vowel pattern words such as *lit - tle,* and *ta - ble.*

5. Have students construct words with color-coded alphabet chips and notice the two parts: *bee - tle, lit - tle, ta - ble.* Review the concept of syllable and how to feel both parts while saying them. Identify *bee* as a double vowel talker, *lit* as closed, and *ta* as open. Identify *tle* and *ble* as C + *le* syllables.

6. Have students place each syllable in the appropriate box on the Vowel Pattern Chart.

Transfer: Using *My Wonderful Aunt, Story Five:*

1. Repeat the activity with words from the story such as *grum - ble.*

2. Have students locate other C + *le* vowel pattern words in the story and verbalize the reasons for their selections.

3. Ask students to brainstorm other C + *le* vowel pattern words that rhyme with the selected words.

Coding lesson: structural analysis
Skill: identification of roots in words
Title: *The Little Yellow Chicken*
Materials: Big Book; Structural Analysis Chart

Procedures:

1. Select a word from the story that contains a root word and an ending such as *cooking.*

2. Write the word *cooking* on the board, making a red box around the *ing.*

3. Explain that the important part of the word is *cook* and that we call this part the *root, base,* or *stem* word.

4. Have students classify *cook* as a root word and write it in the appropriate section of the Structural Analysis Chart.

Transfer:

Using *My Wonderful Aunt, Story Five,* repeat the activity with words

from the story such as *turning* and *eagerly.*

Coding lesson: structural analysis
Skill: identification of suffixes in words
Title: *The Little Yellow Chicken*
Materials: Big Book; Structural Analysis Chart; colored transparent tape or wax-covered yarn; wall charts

Procedures:

1. Select a word from the story that contains a suffix such as *cooking*.

2. Write *cooking* on the board, making a red box around the ing.

3. Review the concept of a root word, explaining the importance of this part.

4. Introduce the term *suffix*, explaining that it is what we add to the end of the base word. We make a red box around the suffix to show that it is a part that is added to the end of the main word.

5. Have students classify the root word and the suffix and write them in the appropriate sections of the Structural Analysis Chart.

Transfer: Using *My Wonderful Aunt, Story Five:*

1. Repeat the activity with words from the story such as *turning* and *delivering*.

2. Have students locate other *ing* words in other stories.

3. Have students use colored transparent tape or wax-covered yarn to indicate the suffix *ing*.

4. Ask students to brainstorm other *ing* words and display them on a wall chart.

3.3 Affixes: Prefixes

Coding lesson: structural analysis

Skill: identification of prefixes in words

Title: *My Wonderful Aunt, Story Five*

Materials: Big Book; Structural Analysis Chart: colored transparent tape or wax-covered yarn

Procedures:

1. Select a word from the story that contains a prefix such as *proclaiming*. (No words with prefixes are used in *The Little Yellow Chicken,* so only *My Wonderful Aunt: Story Five* was used for this lesson.)

2. Write *proclaiming* on the board, making a green box around the prefix *pro*. You might also make a red box around the suffix *ing*.

3. Review the concept of a root word, explaining the importance of this part.

4. Introduce the term *prefix,* explaining that it is what we add to the beginning of the base word. We make a green box around the prefix to show that it is a part that is added to the beginning of the main word.

5. Have students classify the root word and the prefix and write them in the appropriate sections of the Structural Analysis Chart.

Transfer:

1. Repeat the activity with words from other stories and words found on charts around the room.

2. Add words to the chart.

3. Ask students to brainstorm other words with prefixes and display them on the word wall.

Coding lesson: structural analysis
Skill: identification of words within compound words
Title: *The Little Yellow Chicken*
Materials: Big Book; puzzle cards, Structural Analysis Chart; wax-covered yarn, or colored transparent tape

Procedures:

1. Select several compound words from the story such as *himself, grandmother, everything.*

2. Using two large, interconnecting puzzle pieces (previously prepared) demonstrate how some big words are made up of two little words: *him + self = himself; grand + mother = grandmother,* etc.

3. Place the puzzle pieces on a chart or a mobile and display them for easy reference. Compound puzzles may also be used as a center activity.

4. Have students list words in the compound words section of the Structural Analysis Chart.

Transfer: Using *My Wonderful Aunt, Story Five:*

1. Repeat the activity with compound words from the story: *someone, popcorn, something, nightshirt, grandfather, teapot.*

2. Have students visually track for compound words and highlight them with wax-covered yarn or colored transparent tape.

3. Ask students to add words to the chart or mobile.

Coding lesson: structural analysis
Skill: identification of words that make up contractions
Title: *The Little Yellow Chicken*
Materials: Big Book; elbow macaroni; wax-covered yarn

Procedures:

1. Select a contraction from the story, such as *wouldn't.*

2. Write the word *wouldn't* on the board and highlight the apostrophe in red.

3. Write the words *would not* below *wouldn't,* making sure the students notice that the two words *would not* are longer and take up more space that the shortened form, or contraction, *wouldn't.* Highlight the *o* (in *not*) in red.

4. Have students compare the two to discover that the apostrophe takes the place of the *o* (*not*), and the meaning is not changed.

5. Have students create a list of contractions with *not.*

6. Display on a chart or a mobile, using elbow macaroni for the apostrophes.

Transfer:

Using *My Wonderful Aunt, Story Five:*

1. Repeat the activity with contractions from the story: *can't, she's, you've, I'll,* and *that's.*

2. Have students locate contractions in various print materials and highlight them with wax-covered yarn.

3. Ask students to make charts of contractions (using *not, is, have, will*) and display them on the word wall.

Coding lesson: structural analysis

Skill: identification of consonant + *le* syllabication pattern

Title: *The Little Yellow Chicken*

Materials: Big Book; color-coded alphabet chips; Vowel Pattern Chart

Procedures:

1. Select a consonant + *le* vowel pattern word from the story such as *beetle*.

2. Write *beetle* on the board, coding the *le* in red.

3. Explain the concept of a C + *le* vowel pattern: *When a word ends in **le** and there's a consonant before it, we cut the word in half before that consonant.* (**bee-tle**)

4. Demonstrate with other C + *le* words such as *lit - tle,* and *ta - ble.*

5. Have students construct words with color-coded alphabet chips and notice the two parts: *bee - tle, lit - tle, ta - ble.* Review the concept of syllable and the way to feel parts of a word while saying the word. Identify *bee* as a double vowel talker, *lit* as closed and *ta* as open. Identify *tle* and *ble* as C + *le* syllables.

6. Have students place each syllable in the appropriate box on the Vowel Pattern Chart.

Transfer: Using *My Wonderful Aunt, Story Five:*

1. Repeat the activity with words from the story such as *grum - ble.*

2. Have students locate other C + *le* words in other stories and verbalize the reasons for their selections.

3. Ask students to brainstorm other C + *le* words that rhyme with the selected words.

Coding lesson: structural analysis

Skill: identification of VC/CV syllabication pattern

Title: *The Little Yellow Chicken*

Materials: Big Book; Syllabication Chart, index cards and scissors

Procedures:

1. Select several words from the story that follow the VC/CV syllabication pattern, such as *yel - low, par - ty, hun - gry.*

2. Write *yellow* on the board, coding the vowels in red.

3. Spot and dot each vowel, making a dot above each vowel and then connecting the dots.

4. Ask students how many letters (consonants) are between the vowels.

5. Tell students, *When 2 consonants are between the vowels, break between them. (yel - low)*

6. Have students feel the two parts of *yellow* when they say the word. Ask them to write the parts on the Syllabication Chart.

7. Puzzles can be made with index cards so that students might practice cutting big words into little chunks using the VC/CV syllabication pattern.

Transfer: Using *My Wonderful Aunt, Story Five:*

1. Repeat the activity with words from the story: *bur-row, in-to, bet-ter, gar-den, un-der, cac-tus. trum-pets, mus-tard.*

2. Have students make and display a chart or mobile with VC/CV pattern words.

3. Ask the students to make puzzles. Include them as a center activity.

3.8 Syllabication: V/CV

Coding lesson: structural analysis

Skill: identification of V/CV syllabication pattern

Title: *The Little Yellow Chicken*

Materials: Big Book; Syllabication Chart; index cards and scissors: color-coded alphabet chips

Procedures:

1. Select several words from the story that follow the V/CV pattern such as *la - zy, i - dea,* and *o - pen.*

2. Write *lazy* on the board, coding the vowels in red.

3. Spot and dot each vowel, making a dot above each vowel and then connecting the dots.

4. Ask students how many consonants are between the vowels.

5. Tell students, *When one consonant is between the vowels, break before that consonant. (la - zy)*

6. Have students feel the two parts of *lazy* when they say the word. Ask them to write the parts on the Syllabication Chart. Each syllable may be placed in the appropriate section of the Vowel Pattern Chart (open).

7. Puzzles can be made with index cards so that students might practice cutting big words into little chunks using the V/CV syllabication pattern.

Transfer: Using *My Wonderful Aunt, Story Five:*

1. Repeat the activity with words from the story such as *be-longs, mu-sic, pa-pers, ca-pers, de-clared.*

2. Have students use color-coded alphabet chips to construct V/CV words from the story and have students break (segment) words into syllables. Make sure students notice that each syllable contains at least one vowel.

3. Ask students to make and display a chart or mobile with V/CV pattern words.

3.9 Syllabication: VC/V

Coding lesson: structural analysis
Skill: identification of VC/V syllabication pattern
Title: *My Wonderful Aunt, Story Five*
Materials: Big Book; Syllabication Chart; index cards and scissors; color-coded alphabet chips

Procedures:

1. Select a word from the story that follows the VC/V pattern such as: *nev - er* or *ev -er.* (No VC/V words are in *The Little Yellow Chicken* so only *My Wonderful Aunt, Story Five* was used for this pattern.)

2. Write *never* on the board, coding the vowels in red.

3. Spot and dot each vowel, making a dot above each vowel and then connecting the dots.

4. Ask students how many consonants are between the vowels. Review the previous pattern (V/CV). Break before the *v.* Say each part: *ne - ver.*

5. Tell students, *when one consonant is between the vowels, we break after that consonant. (**nev - er**)*

6. Have students feel the two parts of *never* when they say the word. Ask them to write the parts on the Syllabication Chart. Each syllable may be placed in the appropriate section of the Vowel Pattern Chart (*nev* = closed, and *er* = bossy r).

7. Puzzles can be made with index cards so that students might practice cutting big words into little chunks, using the VC/V syllabication pattern. (Note that this version of the VCV pattern occurs much less frequently than the V/CV version.)

Transfer:

1. Repeat the activity with words from other stories or print around the room.

2. Use color-coded alphabet chips to construct VC/V words from the story. Have students break (segment) the words into syllables. Make sure students notice that each syllable contains at least one vowel.

3. Ask students to make and display a chart or mobile with VC/V pattern words.

Level 4

Third Grade-
Fifth Grade

Teacher's Remedial

Assessment Sheets

Level 4 Remedial Assessment and Instructional Matrix

Assessment Component	Subtests
Phonological Awareness	**4.5 Segmenting: Phonemes** **4.8 Blending: Phonemes** **4.9 Phoneme Identification: Initial** **4.10 Phoneme Identification: Final** **4.11 Phoneme Identification: Medial** **4.12 Manipulation: Deletion** **4.13 Manipulation: Substitutions: Initial** **4.14 Manipulation: Substitutions: Final** **4.15 Manipulation: Substitutions: Medial**
Synthetic Phonics	**4.3 Short Vowels** **4.4 Consonant Digraphs** **4.5 Consonant Blends** **4.6 _R_-controlled Vowels** **4.7 Vowel Digraphs** **4.8 Diphthongs** **4.9 Phoneme Segmenting and Blending**

Analytic Phonics	4.2 Word Families: Production
	4.3 Word Families: Substitution of Initial Letter
	4.4 Word Families: Substitution of Final Letter
	4.5 Word Families: Substitution of Medial Letter
Vowel Patterns	4.1 Closed
	4.2 Open
	3.3 Silent *e*
	4.4 Bossy *r*
	4.5 Double Vowel Talkers
	4.6 Double Vowel Whiners
	4.7 Consonant + *le*
Structural Analysis	4.1 Root Words
	4.2 Affixes: Suffixes
	4.3 Affixes: Prefixes
	4.4 Compound Words
	4.5 Contractions
	4.6 Syllabication: C + *le*
	4.7 Syllabication: VC/CV
	4.8 Syllabication: V/CV
	4.9 Syllabication: VC/V

Level 4 Student Profile

Date

Name

Grade   **Teacher**

Examiner

Directions: Mark a + for *passing* and a – for *needs instruction*.

Level 4 Student Profile

Phonological Awareness

Subtest	Pre-	Post-
4.5		
4.8		
4.9		
4.10		
4.11		
4.12		
4.13		
4.14		
4.15		

Synthetic Phonics

Subtest	Pre-	Post-
4.3		
4.4		
4.5		
4.6		
4.7		
4.8		
4.9		

Analytic Phonics

Subtest	Pre-	Post-
4.2		
4.3		
4.4		
4.5		

Vowel Patterns

Subtest	Pre-	Post-
4.1		
4.2		
4.3		
4.4		
4.5		
4.6		

Structural Analysis

Subtest	Pre-	Post-
4.1		
4.2		
4.3		
4.4		
4.5		
4.6		
4.7		
4.8		
4.9		

Directions: Mark a + for a correct response and a – for an incorrect response.
Each subtest has a practice item. The words the teacher says are in italics.
A passing score is 4 correct responses out of 6. If a student misses two or more
items, instruction may be indicated. Correct responses are in parentheses.

Name		Date
Grade	Teacher	
Examiner		

Level 4 Informal Assessment of Phonological Awareness

4.5 Segmenting: Phonemes

I will say a word: **mat.** *Tell me each sound you hear in* **mat.**

Say /m/ - /a/ - /t/ with the student.

see (s - ee)	_____	**ship** (sh - i - p)	_____
do (d - oo)	_____	**side** (s - i - d)	_____
fat (f - a - t)	_____	**city** (s - i - t - ee)	_____

4.8 Blending: Phonemes

Listen while I say some sounds: **/a/ - /t/.** *Now say them together.*

m - e	_____	**s - ea - t**	_____
s - o	_____	**d - o - g**	_____
f - i - sh	_____	**l - u - n - ch**	_____

4.9 Phoneme Identification: Initial

Listen to the beginning sound in the word **soap.** *Say the beginning
sound in the word* **soap.**

milk	_____	**vacuum**	_____
fish	_____	**nest**	_____
zoo	_____	**suit**	_____

Level 4 Informal Assessment of Phonological Awareness (continued)

Directions: Mark a + for a correct response and a − for an incorrect response.

Name		Date
Grade	Teacher	
Examiner		

Level 4 Informal Assessment of Phonological Awareness (continued)

4.10 Phoneme Identification: Final

*Listen to the ending sound in the word **bus**. Tell me the ending sound.*

top	_____	**duck**	_____
pit	_____	**come**	_____
mug	_____	**house**	_____

4.11 Phoneme Identification: Medial

*Listen to the middle sound in the word **meet**. Tell me the middle sound.*

cake	_____	**pat**	_____
boat	_____	**him**	_____
ride	_____	**set**	_____

4.12 Manipulation: Deletion

*Say the word **football**. Say it again but don't say **foot**. Say ball with the student.*

Say the word **houseboat**. Say it again but don't say **house**. (boat) _____

Say the word **tiger**. Say it again but don't say **ti**. (ger) _____

Say the word **coat**. Say it again but don't say **c**. (oat) _____

Say the word **billboard**. Say it again but don't say **board**. (bill) _____

Say the word **table**. Say it again but don't say **ble**. (ta) _____

Say the word **soup**. Say it again but don't say **p**. (sou) _____

Level 4 Informal Assessment of Phonological Awareness (continued)

Directions: Mark a + for a correct response and a − for an incorrect response.

Name		Date
Grade	Teacher	
Examiner		

Level 4 Informal Assessment of Phonological Awareness (continued)

4.13 Manipulation: Substitutions: Initial

Listen while I say the word **hen.** *If I change the* /**h**/ *to* /**p**/**,** *the new word is* **pen.** *Now say the word* **mat.** *Change the* /**m**/ *to* /**s**/. *The new word is _____.* (sat)

Say **hill.** Change the /**h**/ to /**j**/. (Jill) _____

Say **fun.** Change the /**f**/ to /**s**/. (sun) _____

Say **might.** Change the /**m**/ to /**f**/. (fight) _____

Say **pay.** Change the /**p**/ to /**d**/. (day) _____

Say **sit.** Change the /**s**/ to /**f**/. (fit) _____

Say **hop.** Change the /**h**/ to /**t**/. (top) _____

4.14 Manipulation: Substitutions: Final Sounds

Listen while I say the word **hop.** *If I change the* /**p**/ *to* /**g**/, *the new word is* **hog.** *Now say the word* **sat.** *Change the* /**t**/ *to* /**p**/. *The new word is _____.* (sack)

Say **cut.** Change the /**t**/ to /**f**/. (cuff) _____

Say **like.** Change the /**k**/ to /**t**/. (light) _____

Say **bait.** Change the /**t**/ to /**k**/. (bake) _____

Say **plum.** Change the /**m**/ to /**s**/. (plus) _____

Say **mop.** Change the /**p**/ to /**m**/. (mom) _____

Say **cat.** Change the /**t**/ to /**p**/. (cap) _____

Level 4 Informal Assessment of
Phonological Awareness (continued)

Directions: Mark a + for a correct response and a − for an incorrect response.

Level 4 Informal Assessment of Phonological Awareness (continued)

4.15 Manipulation: Substitutions: Medial

*Listen while I say the word **mate.** If I change the /**a**/ to /**i**/, the new word is **might.** Now say the word **seep.** Change the /**ee**/ to /**oa**/. The new word is _____.* (soap)

Say **pet.** Change the /**e**/ to /**i**/. (pit)   _____

Say **cab.** Change the /**a**/ to /**o**/. (cob)   _____

Say **fit.** Change the /**i**/ to /**a**/. (fat)   _____

Say **moon.** Change the /**oo**/ to /**ee**/. (mean)   _____

Say **beat.** Change the /**ea**/ to /**i**/. (bite)   _____

Say **mop.** Change the /**o**/ to /**a**/. (map)   _____

Level 4 Informal Assessment of Synthetic Phonics
(refer to Level 4 Synthetic Phonics Student Sheets)

4.3 Short Vowels

Ask the student to look at each word on the Student Sheet and tell you the vowel sound in the word. Then ask the student to say the word.

Example: cat (/a/)

	Pre-	Post-
pet (/e/)		
hop (/o/)		
man (/a/)		
rug (/u/)		
fish (/i/)		
Score		

Look at these letter. Tell me what sounds they make.

Example: st

4.4 Consonant Digraphs
4.5 Consonant Blends

	Pre-	Post-
sh		
ch		
th		
wh		
ph		
cl		
gr		
st		
bl		
sk		
Score		

4.6 *R*-Controlled Vowels

	Pre-	Post-
ar (/ar/)		
er (/er/)		
ir (/er/)		
or (/or/)		
ur (/er/)		
Score		

261

Level 4 Informal Assessment of Synthetic Phonics

Directions: Mark a + for a correct response and a − for an incorrect response.

Name		Date
Grade	Teacher	
Examiner		

Level 4 Informal Assessment of Synthetic Phonics (continued)

Directions: Mark a + for a correct response and a – for an incorrect response.

Name	Date
Grade	Teacher
Examiner	

Level 4 Informal Assessment of Synthetic Phonics (continued)

(refer to Level 4 Synthetic Phonics Student Sheets)

4.7 Vowel Digraphs

	Pre-	Post-
ai (/ā/)		
ee (/ē/)		
oa (/ō/)		
oe (/ō/)		
ie (/ē/)		
Score		

4.8 Diphthongs

	Pre-	Post-
oy (/oy/)		
ow (/ow/)		
oi (/oi/)		
ou (/ou/)		
Score		

4.9 Phoneme Segmenting and Blending

Sound it out. Now say the whole word.

	Pre-	Post-
m - e (me)		
g - o (go)		
s - a - t (sat)		
f - i - l (fill)		
m - e - n (men)		
n - e - s - t (nest)		
Score		

Level 4 Informal Assessment of Analytic Phonics

(refer to Level 4 Analytic Phonics Student Sheets)

4.2 Word Families: Production

*Write another word in the same word family as **hop** and **top**.* (pop)
Add to these word families.

	Pre-	Post-
tip, lip		
make, bake		
sack, pack		
bell, tell		
dot, hot		
bump, jump		
Score		

4.3 Word Families: Substitution of Initial Letter

*Show the student the word **sit**. Look at the word **sit**. Change the first letter **s** to **b**. Say the new word* (bit) *and write it on the line.*

			Pre-	Post-
top	Change *t* to *m*	(mop)		
lip	Change *l* to *s*	(sip)		
car	Change *c* to *f*	(far)		
boat	Change *b* to *g*	(goat)		
meet	Change *m* to *b*	(beet)		
look	Change *l* to *b*	(book)		
joy	Change *j* to *t*	(toy)		
Score				

Level 4 Informal Assessment of Analytic Phonics

Directions: Mark a + for a correct response and a – for an incorrect response.

Name		Date
Grade	Teacher	
Examiner		

Level 4 Informal Assessment of Analytic Phonics (continued)

Directions: Mark a + for a correct response and a – for an incorrect response.

	Name	Date
	Grade	Teacher
	Examiner	

Level 4 Informal Assessment of Analytic Phonics (continued)

(refer to Level 4 Analytic Phonics Student Sheets)

4.4 Word Families: Substitution of Final Letter

Show student the word **sit**. *Look at the word **sit**. Change the last letter to **p**. Say the new word* (sip) *and write it on the line.*

			Pre-	Post-
lot	Change *t* to *g*	(got)		
pen	Change *n* to *t*	(pet)		
hip	Change *p* to *d*	(hid)		
shot	Change *t* to *p*	(shop)		
plug	Change *g* to *s*	(plus)		
meet	Change *t* to *k*	(meek)		
Score				

4.5 Word Families: Substitution of Medial Letter

Show student the word **sit**. *Look at the word **sit**. Change the middle letter to **a**. Say the new word* (sat) *and write it on the line.*

			Pre-	Post-
make	Change *a* to *i*	(mike)		
ride	Change *i* to *o*	(rode)		
wade	Change *a* to *i*	(wide)		
mud	Change *u* to *a*	(mad)		
ten	Change *e* to *i*	(tin)		
stop	Change *o* to *e*	(step)		
Score				

Level 4 Informal Assessment of Vowel Patterns

(refer to Level 4 Vowel Patterns Student Sheets)

I will show you some nonsense words. Read them to me.

4.1 Closed

	Pre-	Post-
fam		
het		
ish		
ot		
nust		
stim		
Score		

4.2 Open

	Pre-	Post-
bo		
li		
mu		
ta		
ne		
vo		
Score		

4.3 Silent *e*

	Pre-	Post-
nake		
fute		
mive		
pere		
stide		
bose		
Score		

4.4 Bossy *r*

	Pre-	Post-
jart		
gorf		
derp		
kird		
murt		
harb		
Score		

4.5 Double Vowel Talkers

	Pre-	Post-
tain		
leep		
poat		
meab		
boe		
tay		
Score		

4.6 Double Vowel Whiners

	Pre-	Post-
mout		
noy		
pown		
voil		
bawp		
goom		
Score		

4.7 Consonant + *le*

	Pre-	Post-
caple		
durkle		
pubble		
rizzle		
hottle		
tifle		
Score		

Level 4 Informal Assessment of Vowel Patterns

Directions: Mark a + for a correct response and a – for an incorrect response.

Name		Date
Grade	Teacher	
Examiner		

Level 4 Informal Assessment of Structural Analysis

Directions: Mark a + for a correct response and a – for an incorrect response.

		Date
Name		
Grade	**Teacher**	
	Examiner	

Level 4 Informal Assessment of Structural Analysis

(refer to Level 4 Structural Analysis Student Sheets)

4.1 Root Words

*Box in the root word of **runs**. (run)*

		Pre-	Post-
friendly	(friend)		
turning	(turn)		
talking	(talk)		
playful	(play)		
buttons	(button)		
heated	(heat)		
Score			

4.3 Affixes: Prefixes

*Box in the prefix of the word **dislike**. (dis)*

		Pre-	Post-
replay	(re)		
unable	(un)		
preview	(pre)		
rewrite	(re)		
unhappy	(un)		
disappear	(dis)		
Score			

4.2 Affixes: Suffixes

*Box in the suffix of the word **airplanes**. (s)*

		Pre-	Post-
pets	(s)		
books	(s)		
walked	(ed)		
wanted	(ed)		
talking	(ing)		
playing	(ing)		
Score			

(refer to Level 4 Structural Analysis Student Sheets)

4.4 Compound Words

Look at the compound word **milkshake**. *Draw a line between the two parts.* (milk/shake)

		Pre-	Post-
sunshine	(sun/shine)		
doghouse	(dog/house)		
railroad	(rail/road)		
outside	(out/side)		
fireman	(fire/man)		
blackboard	(black/board)		
Score			

4.6 Syllabication: C + *le*

Divide this word into syllables: **apple**. (ap/ple)

		Pre-	Post-
table	(ta/ble)		
bubble	(bub/ble)		
purple	(pur/ple)		
rifle	(ri/fle)		
cycle	(cy/cle)		
puddle	(pud/dle)		
Score			

4.5 Contractions

Write the contraction for the words **can not**. (can't)

		Pre-	Post-
he is	(he's)		
let us	(let's)		
we will	(we'll)		
is not	(isn't)		
I am	(I'm)		
did not	(didn't)		
Score			

Level 4 Informal Assessment of Structural Analysis (continued)

Directions: Mark a + for a correct response and a – for an incorrect response.

Name		Date
Grade	Teacher	
Examiner		

Level 4 Informal Assessment of Structural Analysis (continued)

Date

Name

Grade   Teacher

Examiner

Directions: Mark a + for a correct response and a − for an incorrect response.

Level 4 Informal Assessment of Structural Analysis (continued)

(refer to Level 4 Structural Analysis Student Sheets)

4.7 Syllabication: VC/CV

Divide this word into syllables: **summer**.
(sum/mer)

		Pre-	Post-
winter	(win/ter)		
basket	(bas/ket)		
better	(bet/ter)		
after	(af/ter)		
ladder	(lad/der)		
signal	(sig/nal)		
Score			

4.8 Syllabication: V/CV

Divide this word into syllables: **robot**.
(ro/bot)

		Pre-	Post-
hotel	(ho/tel)		
diver	(di/ver)		
tiger	(ti/ger)		
music	(mu/sic)		
bacon	(ba/con)		
paper	(pa/per)		
Score			

4.9 Syllabication: VC/V

Divide this word into syllables: **panic**.
(pan/ic)

		Pre-	Post-
cabin	(cab/in)		
wagon	(wag/on)		
dragon	(drag/on)		
robin	(rob/in)		
lemon	(lem/on)		
melon	(mel/on)		
Score			

Level 4

Third Grade-
Fifth Grade

Student Assessment
Sheets

Level 4 Synthetic Phonics Student Sheet

4.3 Short Vowels

p<u>e</u>t   h<u>o</u>p   m<u>a</u>n

r<u>u</u>g   f<u>i</u>sh

4.4 Consonant Digraphs

sh   ch   th   wh   ph

4.5 Consonant Blends

cl   gr   st   bl   sk

Level 4 Synthetic Phonics Student Sheet (continued)

4.6 *R*-Controlled Vowels

ar   er   ir   or   ur

4.7 Vowel Digraphs

ai   ee   oa   oe   ie

4.8 Diphthongs

oy   ow   oi   ou

4.9 Phoneme Segmenting and Blending

Practice item: **no**

---

me   go   sat   fill   men   nest

Practice item:

hop	top	_____

---

tip	lip	_____
make	bake	_____
sack	pack	_____
bell	tell	_____
dot	hot	_____
bump	jump	_____

4.3 Word Families: Substitution of Initial Letter

Practice item:

sit	**Change *s* to *b***	_____

top	**Change *t* to *m***	_____
lip	**Change *l* to *s***	_____
car	**Change *c* to *f***	_____
boat	**Change *b* to *g***	_____
meet	**Change *m* to *b***	_____
look	**Change *l* to *b***	_____
joy	**Change *j* to *t***	_____

Practice item:

sit	Change *t* to *p*	_____

lot	Change *t* to *g*	_____
pen	Change *n* to *t*	_____
hip	Change *p* to *d*	_____
shot	Change *t* to *p*	_____
plug	Change *g* to *b*	_____
meet	Change *m* to *k*	_____

Practice item:

sit	**Change *i* to *a***	_____

---

make	**Change *a* to *i***	_____
ride	**Change *i* to *o***	_____
wade	**Change *a* to *i***	_____
mud	**Change *u* to *a***	_____
ten	**Change *e* to *i***	_____
stop	**Change *o* to *e***	_____

Level 4 Vowel Patterns Student Sheet

4.1 Closed

fam	**ot**
het	**nust**
ish	**stim**

4.2 Open

bo	**ta**
li	**ne**
mu	**vo**

4.3 Silent *e*

nake   pere

fute   stide

mive   bose

4.4 Bossy *r*

jart   kird

gorf   murt

derp   harb

4.5 Double Vowel Talkers

tain   meab

leep   boe

poat   tay

4.6 Double Vowel Whiners

mout   voil

noy   bawp

pown   goom

caple	**rizzle**
durkle	**hottle**
pubble	**tifle**

Level 4 Structural Analysis Student Sheet

4.1 Root Words

Practice item:

runs

---

friendly   **playful**

turning   **buttons**

talking   **heated**

Practice item:

airplanes

---

pets   books

walked   wanted

talking   playing

4.3 Affixes: Prefixes

Practice item:
dislike

---

replay   **preview**   **unhappy**

unable   **rewrite**   **disappear**

4.4 Compound Words

Practice item:
milkshake

---

sunshine   **outside**

doghouse   **fireman**

railroad   **blackboard**

Practice item:

can not   _____

_____

he is   _____

let us   _____

we will   _____

is not   _____

I am   _____

did not   _____

4.6 Syllabication: C + *le*

Practice item:
apple

---

table	**purple**	**cycle**
bubble	**rifle**	**puddle**

4.7 Syllabication: VC/CV

Practice item:
summer

---

winter	**better**	**ladder**
basket	**after**	**signal**

4.8 Syllabication: V/CV

Practice item:

robot

---

hotel	tiger	bacon
diver	music	paper

4.9 Syllabication: VC/V

Practice item:

panic

---

cabin	dragon	lemon
wagon	robin	melon

Level 4

Third Grade–
Fifth Grade

Remedial Lessons

Level 4 Prototype Lessons

Level 4 Prototype Lessons

Level 4 Remedial Lessons

Any of the lesson plans from Level 2 or Level 3 can be used for remedial teaching. In addition, following are lesson plan grids for remedial teaching that identify vocabulary from two books that can be used to replace vocabulary in lesson plans for prior levels. The books used are the following:

The Number Cruncher by Judy Gilbert (SUNSHINE™, The Wright Group)

Time Warp by John Lockyer (SUNSHINE™, The Wright Group)

Blackline masters are provided in Appendix 1 for use in developing lesson plans.

Coding Lesson: phonological awareness

Procedures: Use prototype lessons 3.5, 3.8, 3.9–3.11 for specific activities. Following are suggested words to be used for these activities.

	The Number Cruncher				*Time Warp*			
4.5/4.8 Segmenting and blending of phonemes	it (i-t) he (h-e) to (t-o) as (a-s) thin (th-in)	come (c-o-m-e) with (w-i-t-h) him (h-i-m) let (l-e-t) gave (g-a-v-e)			not (n-o-t) can (c-a-n) sir (s-i-r) log (l-o-g) deck (d-e-c-k)	fact (f-a-c-t) over (o-v-e-r) time (t-i-m-e) last (l-a-s-t) little (l-i-t-t-l-e)		
4.9 Phoneme identification: initial	(w) wonder with was	(s)	seventh surprise special		(n) not no negative	(f)	fact failed first	
	(b) bed brother busy	(t)	talk time twelve		(b) being buzzed blared	(p)	primitive panel petrak	
4.10 Phoneme identification: final	(t) went night put	(er)	number cruncher wonder		(t) foot sit lit	(d)	speed around flashed	
	(d) bed mumbled said	(p)	asleep help stop		(p) spaceship up snap	(n)	screen can sign	
4.11 Phoneme identification: medial	(i) did six is	(ee)	need squeeky asleep		(e) let negative Jensen	(l)	him his lit	
	(e) let went fell bed	(a)	gave late make take		(a) pad stamped panel	(ee)	screen see repeat	

Coding Lesson: phonological awareness

Procedures: Use prototype lessons 3.12–3.15 for specific activities. Following are suggested words to be used for these activities.

	The Number Cruncher	*Time Warp*
4.12 Manipulation: deletions	whispered whisper years year hardly hard slices slice jumped jump glowed glow	alarms alarm sitting sit drifted drift channels channel getting get shouted shout
4.13 Manipulation: substitutions of initial sounds	him tim dim rim did hid lid rid can man tan fan met set let get	he me tea see be lit mit pit fit wit pad lad mad sad fad can pan tan fan Dan time dime lime mine
4.14 Manipulation: substitutions of final sounds	his hit him hid did dim dip dill can cap cat cab met men mess Meg	it is in ten ted dip did din dig tap tan tad tab look loot loop loom
4.15 Manipulation: substitutions of medial sounds	full fill fall fell let lot lit did dad dead will well wall	stop not nut net tap tip top log leg lag

Coding Lesson: synthetic phonics

Procedures: Use prototype lessons 3.1–3.5 for specific activities. Following are suggested words to be used for these activities.

	The Number Cruncher		*Time Warp*	
4.1 Consonants	(b) birthday bed, button (g) grandpa gadgets getting gave	(p) pajama pushed paper piece (n) number nearly night nine	(d) door duty date distress (t) touched tried turned	(p) panel Petrak primitive pad (f) first fleet fact
4.2 Long vowels	(a) make gave paper take (e) be me we between	(i) tiny surprise night right (o) woke over old home	(a) space snapped rated (e) report he response	(i) unidentified quite computer- ization sign (o) open hole no those
4.3 Short vowels	(e) getting them let bed (a) gadgets thanks rather	(i) his with thin (u) but button up number	(e) step Jensen sensor entered (i) his slid sitting	(a) panel pad another black (u) up hunched but
4.4 Consonant digraphs	(wh) what when (th) seventh birthday grandfather thin that the thirty	(ch) teacher cruncher lunches children (sh) pushed	(th) through the another (sh) shook flashed spaceship shouted	(ch) punched channels touched (wh) who what everywhere

Coding lesson: synthetic phonics

Procedures: Use prototype lessons 3.6–3.9 for specific activities. Following are suggested words to be used for these activities.

	The Number Cruncher	*Time Warp*
4.5 Consonant blends	(gr) grandfather (sp) special great (pr) presents (sl) slices surprise asleep (cl) clever (br) bread (dr) drew (st) stopped	(st) stamped (fr) front stairway frowned studied (bl) black (sp) speed blackened space (sn) snapped (sl) slid (fl) fleet
4.6 *R*-controlled vowels	*er:* birthday, grandfather, wonder, clever, calculator, words, number, cruncher *ear:* nearly, hear, years *ar:* dark, hardly *or:* your, more, four, for, fourteen	*er:* turned, officer, over, earth, sensor, sir, clear, years *ear:* clear, years, appeared *ar:* are, markings, star *or:* disturbed, warp, forms, force
4.7 Vowel digraphs	birthday, always, screen, asleep, away, squeaky, wait, need, each, day, quiet, leaves, three, feet, tree	wailed, giant, screen, tried, fleet, see, repeat, speed, failed, aboard, ailing, decreasing, beam, streaked, weakly, rain
4.8 Diphthongs	foot, to, voice, about, school afternoon, how, room, new, counted, drew, houses	foot, council, all, drowned, pointed, drowned, around, out, frowned, looked, own, paused, humanoid, now
4.9 Phoneme segmenting and blending	to (t-o) let (l-e-t) it (i-t) said (s-a-i-d) is (i-s) put (p-u-t) in (i-n) time (t-i-m-e) up (u-p) did (d-i-d) do (d-o) can (c-a-n)	made (m-a-d-e) pad (p-a-d) over (o-v-e-r) lit (l-i-t) not (n-o-t) date (d-a-t-e) with (w-i-t-h) star (s-t-a-r) life (l-i-f-e) deck (d-e-c-k) fact (f-a-c-t) mode (m-o-d-e)

4.2-4.5 Analytic Phonics

Coding Lesson: analytic phonics		
Procedures: Use prototype lessons 3.2–3.5 for specific activities. Following are suggested words to be used for these activities.		
	The Number Cruncher	*Time Warp*
4.2 Production	ay: always, birthday, day ell: fell, well, bell ed: bed ight:night, right at: that an: can, than, began all: call, tall	ay: stairway, bay ell: tell ack:black, back ight:lights, tight an: can, commander, channel ar: star, part, cargo, marks og: log ip: dip, ship
4.3 Substitution of initial letter	bed, Ted, fed, led cat, fat, mat, pat, sat fell, tell, well, sell can, pan, tan, fan wait, bait day, bay, say, may	pad, pat, pan lit, lip, lid tap, tad, tack, tab can, cap, cat, cab dip, dim, dig
4.4 Substitution of final letter	his, hit, him cat, cap, can did, dip, dim big, bit, bib	lit, lip, lid tap, tad, tack, tab can, cap, cat, cab dip, dim, dig
4.5 Substitution of middle letter	fell, fill, full, fall will, well, wall ten, tin, ton bell, bill, ball	pad, pod will, wall, well tap, tip, top lock, lack, lick

4.1–4.7 Vowel Patterns

Coding Lesson: vowel patterns		
Procedures: Use prototype lessons 3.1–3.7 for specific activities. Following are suggested words to be used for these activities.		
	The Number Cruncher	*Time Warp*
4.1 Closed	his, with, up, math, them, thin, let, went, bed, fell, cat, can, yes, plus	up, slid, pad, lit, craft, can, log, black, back, last, ship, just, ten, lost, drift
4.2 Open	he, I, me, she, by, we, go, be, my	he, no, I
4.3 Silent *e*	gave, late, woke, time, make, lines, home, nine, five, wide	space, hole, time, made, life, those, date, five, nose, like, file, drive
4.4 Bossy *r*	dark, turn, for, first	her, sir, first, star, forms, turned, warp
4.5 Double vowel talkers	screen, wait, need, each, day, clean, feet, road, own, way, tree	speed, screen, see, shook, tried, fleet, ear, beam, wailed, clear
4.6 Double vowel whiners	room, out, school, how, new, drew, count, took, found	foot, now, out, pointed, too, frowned
4.7 C + *le*	mumbled	little, simple

Coding Lesson: structural analysis

Procedures: Use prototype lessons 3.1–3.5 for specific activities. Following are suggested words to be used for these activities.

	The Number Cruncher	*Time Warp*
4.1 Root words	teacher inventing glowed pushed hardly longer nearly cruncher exactly	stamped drifted suddenly commander
4.2 Affixes: suffixes	inventing glowed pushed hardly longer nearly teacher cruncher exactly	stamped drifted suddenly commander
4.3 Affixes: prefixes	N/A	unidentified
4.4 Compound words	birthday grandfather anything himself chalkboard	stairway spaceship anything starlog
4.5 Contractions	I'll, it's, let's, didn't, I've, that's	didn't, I'm, we're, can't

Coding Lesson: structural analysis

Procedures: Use prototype lesson 3.6–3.9 for specific activities. Following are suggested words to be used for these activities.

	The Number Cruncher	*Time Warp*
4.6 Syllabication: C + *le*	mum-ble	lit-tle sim-ple
4.7 Syllabication: VC/CV	ob-long sur-prise but-ton thir-ty hun-dred fif-ty sis-ter crun-cher twen-ty un-til gar-dens	com-man-der sud-den-ly sen-sor chan-nels drif-ted com-mand sec-tor sig-nal af-ter Jen-sen scan-ner con-tact per-haps
4.8 Syllabication: V/CV	ti-ny pa-per be-gan o-ver se-cret	re-port du-ty re-sponse o-ver re-peat hu-man di-ving de-nied
4.9 Syllabication: VC/V	clev-er pres-ent sev-enth	pan-el nev-er stat-ic

Appendices

Appendix 1: Reproducibles for Lesson Plans

- Code It—Phonological Awareness
- Code It—Print Awareness
- Code It—Graphophonic Analysis: Synthetic Phonics
- Code It—Graphophonic Analysis: Analytic Phonics
- Code It—Graphophonic Analysis: Vowel Patterns
- Code It—Structural Analysis
- Lesson Plan Format
- Vowel Pattern Chart
- Structural Analysis Chart
- Syllabication Chart

Appendix 2: Texts Used in Lesson Plans

- **Level 1:**

  Jack and Jill

  Little Boy Blue

- **Level 2:**

  Down by the Bay

  Annabel

- **Level 3:**

  The Little Yellow Chicken

  My Wonderful Aunt, Story Five

- **Level 4:**

  The Number Cruncher

  Time Warp

Coding lesson: phonological awareness

Objective:

Title:

Materials:

Procedures:

Follow-up:

Coding lesson: print awareness
Objective:
Title:
Materials:
Procedures:
Follow-up:

Coding lesson: synthetic phonics

Objective:

Title:

Materials:

Procedures:

Follow-up:

Coding lesson: analytic phonics

Objective:

Title:

Materials:

Procedures:

Follow-up:

Coding lesson: vowel patterns
Objective:
Title:
Materials:
Procedures:
Follow-up:

Coding lesson: structural analysis

Objective:

Title:

Materials:

Procedures:

Follow-up:

Title:		
Process	**Materials**	**Activity**
Preread it		
Read it		
Reread it		
Discuss it		
React to it		
Code it		
Apply it		
Transfer it		

Vowel Pattern Chart

Closed	Open	Silent e

Bossy *r*	Two Vowels		C + *le*
	Talkers	Whiners	

Structural Analysis Chart

Prefixes	Root words	Suffixes	Compound words	Contractions

C + le	VC/CV	VCV	
		V/CV	VC/V

Syllabication Chart

Level 1

Jack and Jill
Traditional

Jack and Jill went up the hill
to fetch a pail of water.
Jack fell down and broke his crown
and Jill came tumbling after.

Up Jack got and home did trot,
as fast as he could caper.
Jack went to bed and covered his head
with vinegar and brown paper.

Rhyming words:
Jill, hill
down, crown
got, trot
bed, head

Words with the same beginning sound:
Jack, Jill
went, water, with
fetch, fell, fast
could, caper, covered
broke, brown
home, head, he

Little Boy Blue
Traditional

Little Boy Blue,
Come blow your horn.
The sheep's in the meadow.
The cow's in the corn.
Where is the boy
Who looks after the sheep?
He's under a haystack,
Fast asleep.

Rhyming words:
horn, corn
sheep, asleep

Words with the same beginning sound:
Boy, Blue, blow
cows, corn, come

Level 2

Down by the Bay

Traditional
(The Song Box®, The Wright Group)

Down by the bay,
(down by the bay)
where the watermelons grow,
(where the watermelons grow)
back to my home,
(back to my home)
I dare not go.
(I dare not go)
For if I do,
(for if I do)
my mother will say,
(my mother will say)
"Did you ever see a bear
combing his hair?"
Down by the bay.

Did you ever see a bee
with a sunburned knee?

Did you ever see a whale
with a polka dot tail?

Did you ever see a moose
kissing a goose?

Did you ever see…

Annabel

By Joy Cowley
(The Story Basket®, The Wright Group)

(Excerpt)
There once was a girl called Annabel.
There once was a girl called Annabel.
Anna, Anna, bel, bel, bel.
Anna, Anna, bel, bel, bel.
There once was a girl called Annabel.

She went out shopping with her crocodile.
She went out shopping with her crocodile.
Croco, croco, dile, dile, dile.
Croco, croco, dile, dile, dile.
She went out shopping with her crocodile.

She bought a bottle of pink shampoo.
She bought a bottle of pink shampoo.
Pink sham, pink sham, poo, poo, poo.
Pink sham, pink sham, poo, poo, poo.
She bought a bottle of pink shampoo.

Level 3

The Little Yellow Chicken
By Joy Cowley
(SUNSHINE™, The Wright Group)

(Excerpt)
The little yellow chicken
thought he'd have a party.
He said to his friends,
"Will you help me
do the shopping?"

His friends laughed at him.

"Hop it!" said the frog.
"Buzz off!" said the bee.
And the big brown beetle
said, "Stop bugging me!"

So the little yellow chicken
went shopping by himself.

When the shopping was done,
the little yellow chicken
said to his friends,
"Will you help me
do the cooking?"

His friends shook their heads.

"Hop it!" said the frog.
"Buzz off!" said the bee.
And the big brown beetle
said, "Stop bugging me!"

So the little yellow chicken
did the cooking by himself.

My Wonderful Aunt, Story Five
By Margaret Mahy
(SUNSHINE™, The Wright Group)

(Excerpt)
Did I ever mention
my wonderful aunt?
She wouldn't say, "No!"
And she wouldn't say, "Can't!"

She lived in a burrow
dug into the ground.
When she wanted to hide,
she could never be found.

But when she came out,
there were always surprises,
and visitors came
in amazing disguises.

The neighbors declared,
"We can't do our work, as
she's turning the neighborhood
into a circus."

Level 4

The Number Cruncher

By Judy Gilbert
(SUNSHINE™, The Wright Group)

(Excerpt)
Jamie loved getting birthday presents
from his grandfather.
It was exciting to wonder what Grandpa
would come up with.
He was always inventing clever gadgets
and machines.
Jamie's room was full of them.

On his seventh birthday,
Jamie's father gave him
a tiny calculator.
It was oblong and nearly as thin
as a piece of paper.
When Jamie pushed the on button,
the words *Number Cruncher* glowed
on the small screen.
"Thanks, Grandpa," said Jamie.
"But what does a number cruncher do?"
"I'll let the number cruncher
surprise you," Grandpa said.
"It is rather special."

Time Warp

By John Lockyer
(SUNSHINE™, The Wright Group)

(Excerpt)
Commander Lenco stamped his foot, urging the conveyor stairway to speed up. Around him, emergency alarms wailed and flashed. The stairway stopped and doors slid open. Commander Lenco stepped onto Space City Gula's observation deck. "Emergency report, Lieutenant," he snapped to the duty officer sitting in front of the giant screen.

The duty officer, Lieutenant Jensen, touched a sensor pad on the panel in front of her. The screen lit up. The lieutenant touched another sensor pad. A spaceship drifted into view on the screen.

"Unidentified craft entered Gula space through black hole in sector 58," Jensen said.

Commander Lenco studied the spaceship. "Contact made?"

Jensen shook her head. "Negative, sir. All frequency channels tried. No response."

Bibliography

Adams, M. J. 1990. *Beginning to Read: Thinking and Learning About Print*. Cambridge, Mass.; MIT Press.

Adams, M. J. 1991. Why not phonics and whole language? In *All language and the creation of literacy* (pp. 40–53), ed. W. Ellis. Baltimore, Md.; The Orton Dyslexia Society.

Adams, M. J. 1994. The progress of the whole-language debate. *Educational Psychologist* 29:217–222.

Adams, M. J., and M. Bruck. 1995. Resolving the 'great debate.' *American Educator* 19 (7); 10–20.

Anderson, R. C., E. H. Hiebert, J. A. Scott, and I. A. Wilkinson. 1985. *Becoming a Nation of Readers: The Report of the Commission on Reading*. Washington, D.C.: National Institute of Education.

Au, K. H., and J. A. Scheu. 1996. Journey toward holistic instruction: Supporting teachers' growth. *The Reading Teacher* 49:468-477.

Beck, I. L., and C. Juel. 1992. The role of decoding in learning to read. In *What Research Has to Say About Reading Instruction*, eds. S. J. Samuels and A. E. Farstrup. Newark, Del.: International Reading Association.

Bergeron, B. S. 1990. What does the term *whole language* mean? Constructing a definition from the literature. *Journal of Reading Behavior* 22:301–329.

Bradley, L., and P. E. Bryant. 1983. Categorizing sounds and learning to read: A causal connection. *Nature* 30:419–421.

Byrne, B., and R. Fielding-Barnsley. 1991. Evaluation of a program to teach phonemic awareness to young children. *Journal of Educational Psychology* 83:451–455.

Calfee, R. C., P. Lindamood, and C. Lindamood. 1973. Acoustic-phonetic skills and reading—kindergarten through twelfth grade. *Journal of Educational Psychology* 64:293–298.

Chall, J. S. 1967, 1983, 1989. *Learning to Read: The Great Debate*. New York: McGraw-Hill.

Chall, J. S., and H. M. Popp. 1996. *Teaching and Assessing Phonics*. Cambridge, Mass.: Educators Publishing Service.

Choate, J. 1995. *Curriculum-Based Assessment and Programming* (3d ed.). New York: Allyn and Bacon.

Clay, M. M., ed. 1979. *The Early Detection of Reading Difficulties: A Diagnostic Survey with Recovery Procedures*. Portsmouth, N.H.: Heinemann.

Clay, M. M. 1991. *Becoming Literate: The Construction of Inner Control*. Portsmouth, N.H.: Heinemann.

Cunningham, P. M. 1995. *Phonics They Use: Words for Reading and Writing* (2d ed.). New York: HarperCollins College Publishers.

Cunningham, P. M., and J. W. Cunningham. 1992. Making words: Enhancing the invented spelling-decoding connection. *The Reading Teacher* 46:106–114.

Dechant, E. 1991. *Understanding and Teaching Reading*. Hillsdale, N.J.: Lawrence Erlbaum Associates.

Dechant, E. 1993. *Whole-Language Reading*. Lancaster, Penn.: Technomic.

Ehri, L. C. 1989. The development of spelling knowledge and its role on reading acquisition and reading disability. *Journal of Learning Disabilities* 22:356–365.

Ehri, L. C. 1991. Learning to read and spell words. In *Learning to Read* (pp. 57–73), eds. L. Rieben and C. A. Perfetti. Hillsdale, N.J.: Lawrence Erlbaum Associates.

Ehri, L. C. 1997. Sight word learning in normal readers and dyslexics. In *Foundations of Reading Acquisition and Dyslexia: Implications for Early Intervention* (pp. 163-189), ed. B. Blachman. Mahwah, N.J.: Lawrence Erlbaum Associates.

Eldredge, J. L. 1995. *Teaching Decoding in Holistic Classrooms*. Englewood Cliffs, N.J.: Merrill.

Fischer, P. E. 1993. *The Sounds and Spelling Patterns of English*. Morrill, Me.: Oxton House Publishers.

Foorman, B. R., D. J. Francis, S. E. Shaywitz, B. A. Shaywitz, and J. M. Fletcher. 1997. The case for early reading intervention. In *Foundations of Reading Acquisition and Dyslexia: Implications for Early Intervention* (pp. 243-264), ed. B. Blachman. Mahwah, N.J.: Lawrence Erlbaum Associates.

Fountas, I. C., and I. L. Hannigan. 1989. Making sense of whole language. *Childhood Education* 65:133–137.

Freppon, P. A., and K. L. Dahl. 1991. Learning about phonics in a whole language classroom. *Language Arts* 68:190–197.

Gagne, E. D., C. W. Yekovich, and F. R. Yekovich. 1993. *The Cognitive Psychology of School Learning* (2d ed.). New York: HarperCollins College Publishers.

Goswami, U. 1986. Children's use of analogy in learning to read: A developmental study. *Journal of Experimental Child Psychology* 42:73–83.

Goswami, U., and F. Mead. 1992. Onset and rime awareness and analogies in reading. *Reading Research Quarterly* 27:153–162.

Griffith, P. L., and M. W. Olson. 1992. Phonemic awareness helps beginning readers break the code. *The Reading Teacher* 45:516–523.

Heymsfeld, C. R. 1989. Filling the hole in whole language. *Educational Leadership* 46:65–68.

Hiebert, E. H., and B. M. Taylor, eds. 1994. *Getting Reading Right from the Start: Effective Early Literacy Interventions.* Boston: Allyn & Bacon.

Honig, B. 1996. *Teaching Our Children to Read: The Role of Skills in a Comprehensive Reading Program.* Thousand Oaks, Calif.: Corwin Press.

International Reading Association. 1998. Learning to read and write: Developmentally appropriate practices for young children. A joint position statement of the IRA and the NAEYC, adopted May 1998. *The Reading Teacher* 52 (2):193–214.

Just, M. A., and P. A. Carpenter. 1987. *The Psychology of Reading and Language Comprehension.* Boston, Mass.: Allyn and Bacon.

The Learning First Alliance. 1998. Every child reading: An action plan of The Learning First Alliance. *American Educator* (Spring/Summer).

Lindamood, C. H., and P. C. Lindamood. 1984. *Auditory Discrimination in Depth.* Austin, Tex.: Pro-Ed.

Lindamood, P. C., and P. D. Lindamood. 1998. *The Lindamood Phoneme Sequencing Program for Reading, Spelling, and Speech (LiPS).* Austin, Tex.: Pro-Ed.

Lundberg, I., J. Frost, and O. Petersen. 1988. Effects of an extensive program for stimulating phonological awareness in preschool children. *Reading Research Quarterly* 23:263–284.

Marzano, R., D. Pickering, and J. McTighe. 1993. *Assessing Student Outcomes: Performance Assessment Using the Dimensions of Learning Model.* Alexandria, Va.: Association for Supervision and Curriculum Development.

Matson, B. 1996. Whole language or phonics? Teachers and researchers find the middle ground most fertile. *The Harvard Education Letter XII* (2):1–5.

May, F. B. 1998. *Reading as Communication* (5th ed.). Columbus, Ohio: Merrill.

McGuinness, D., C. McGuinness, and J. Donohue. 1995. Phonological training and the alphabet principle: Evidence for reciprocal causality. *Reading Research Quarterly* 30:830–852.

McKenna, M. C., R. D. Robinson, and J. W. Miller. 1990. Whole language: A research agenda for the nineties. *Educational Researcher* 19:3–6.

McKenna, M. C., R. D. Robinson, and J. W. Miller. 1994. Whole language and research: The case for caution. In *Whole Language: The Debate* (pp. 17–42), (report no. CS 011 581), moderator C. B. Smith, Bloomington, Ind.: ERIC Clearinghouse on Reading, English, and Communication (ERIC Document Reproduction No. ED 366 905).

Mills, H., T. O'Keefe, and D. Stephens. 1990. *Looking Closer: The Role of Phonics in a Whole Language Classroom.* Urbana, Ill.: National Council of Teachers of English.

Moats, L. C. 1998. Teaching decoding. *American Educator* 22:42–49.

Moustafa, M. 1997. *Beyond Traditional Phonics.* Portsmouth, N.H.: Heinemann.

Myklebust, H. 1965. *Development and Disorders of Written Language* (Vol. 1). New York: Grune and Stratton.

Payne, D. A. 1997. *Applied Educational Assessment.* Belmont, Calif.: Wadsworth Publishing Company.

Pike, K., R. Compain, and J. Mumper. 1997. *New Connections: An Integrated Approach to Literacy* (2d ed.). Menlo Park, Calif.: Addison-Wesley/Longman.

Pressley, M. 1994. Commentary on the ERIC whole language debate. In *Whole Language: The Debate* (pp. 187–217) (report no. CS 011 581), moderator C. B. Smith. Bloomington, Ind.: ERIC Clearinghouse on Reading, English, and Communication (ERIC Document Reproduction Service No. ED 366 905).

Reutzel. D., and R. Cooter. 1996. *Teaching Children to Read.* Columbus, Ohio: Merrill.

Robertson, C., and W. Salter. 1995a. *The Phonological Awareness Kit.* East Moline, Ill.: LinguiSystems.

Robertson, C., and W. Salter. 1995b. *The Phonological Awareness Test.* East Moline, Ill.: LinguiSystems.

Robinson, R. 1994. "Let us not permit ourselves to be forced into bitterly polarized positions..." In *Whole Language: The Debate* (pp. 62–64) (report no. CS 011 581), moderator C. B. Smith. Bloomington, Ind.: ERIC Clearinghouse on Reading, English, and Communication (ERIC Document Reproduction Service No. ED 366 905).

Routman, R. 1991. *Invitations.* Portsmouth, N.H.: Heinemann.

Routman, R. 1996. *Literacy at the Crossroads.* Portsmouth, N.H.: Heinemann.

Share, D. L., and K. E. Stanovich. 1995. Cognitive processes in early reading development: A model of acquisition and individual differences. *Issues in Education: Contributions from Educational Psychology* 1:1–57.

Smith, F. 1988. *Understanding Reading: A Psycholinguistic Analysis of Reading and Learning to Read.* Hillsdale, N.J.: Lawrence Erlbaum Associates.

Stahl, S. A. 1992. Saying the "p" word: Nine guidelines for exemplary phonics instruction. *The Reading Teacher* 45:618–625.

Stahl, S. A., M. C. McKenna, and J. R. Pagnucco. 1994. The effects of whole-language: An update and a reappraisal. *Educational Psychologist* 29:175–185.

Stanovich, K. E. 1986. Matthew effects on reading: Some consequences of individual differences in the acquisition of literacy. *Reading Research Quarterly* 21:360–407.

Strickland, D. S. 1998. *Teaching Phonics Today: A Primer for Educators.* Newark, Del.: International Reading Association.

Teale, B. 1991. Dear readers. *Language Arts* 68:184–187.

Torgesen, J. K. 1998. Catch them before they fall: Identification and assessment to prevent reading failure in young children. *American Educator* 22 (1-2):32–39.

Torgesen, J. K., and B. Bryant. 1993. *Phonological Awareness Training for Reading.* Austin, Tex.: Pro-Ed.

Torgeson, J. K., and B. Bryant. 1994. *Test of Phonological Awareness.* Austin, Tex.: Pro-Ed.

Torgeson, J. K., R. K. Wagner, and C. A. Rashotte. 1994. Longitudinal studies of phonological processing and reading. *Journal of Learning Disabilities* 27: 276–286.

Trachtenberg, P. 1990. Using children's literature to enhance phonics instruction. *The Reading Teacher* 43: 648–652.

Truch, S. 1998. *Phonological Processing, Reading, and the Lindamood Phoneme Sequencing Program: A Review of Related Research.* Austin, Tex.: Pro-Ed.

Tunmer, W. E. 1991. Phonological awareness and literacy acquisition. In *Learning to Read* (pp. 105–119), eds. L. Rieben and C. A. Perfetti. Hillsdale, N.J.: Lawrence Erlbaum Associates.

Tunmer, W. E., and J. Chapman. 1996. Language prediction skill, phonological recoding ability, and beginning reading. In *Reading and Spelling: Development and Disorder*, eds. C. Hulme and R. M. Joshi. Mahwah, N.J.: Lawrence Erlbaum Associates.

Tunmer, W. E., M. L. Herriman, and A. R. Nesdale. 1988. Metalinguistic abilities and beginning reading. *Reading Research Quarterly* 23: 134–158.

Uhry, J. K., and M. J. Shepherd. 1997. Teaching phonological recoding to young children with phonological processing deficits: The effect on sight-vocabulary acquisition. *Learning Disability Quarterly* 20: 104–125.

Vail, P. L. 1991. *Common Ground: Whole Language and Phonics Working Together.* Rosemont, N.J.: Modern Learning Press.

Valencia, S., E. Hiebert, and P. Afflerbach, eds. 1994. *Authentic Reading Assessment: Practices and Possibilities.* Newark, Del.: International Reading Association.

Wylie, R. E., and D. D. Durrell. 1970. *Elementary English* 47:787–791.

Yopp, H. K. 1992. Developing phonemic awareness in young children. *The Reading Teacher* 45 (9):696–703.

Yopp, H. K. 1995. A test for assessing phonemic awareness in young children. *The Reading Teacher* 49: 20–29.

Yopp, H. K., and R. H. Yopp. 1997. *Oo-ples and Boo-noo-noos: Songs and Activities for Phonemic Awareness.* Orlando, Fla.: Harcourt Brace.

Zaragoza, N. 1997. *Rethinking Language Arts: Passion and Practice.* New York: Garland Publishing.

Glossary

affix One or more letters or sounds that occur before or after a base word and which changes the meaning or grammatical function of the word; a prefix or suffix

analytic phonics An instructional approach that introduces whole words and encourages students to discover letter-sound relationships

compound word A word that is composed of two words that can stand alone (e.g., *fireman, doghouse*)

contraction A single word formed by combining two words and deleting one or more letters, with an apostrophe in place of the deleted letter(s) (e.g., *can't, I'm*)

explicit instruction A direct approach to teaching key concepts and skills outside the context of meaningful reading or writing

grapheme The visual representation or symbol of a sound or phoneme

graphophonic analysis The process of decoding new words by using recognizable patterns in known words

implicit instruction An indirect approach to teaching key concepts and skills within the context of meaningful reading and writing

in-context instruction Instruction that is done within the context of meaningful reading and/or writing experiences

onset/rime The *onset* is the initial consonant sound of a word or syllable (e.g., *f* in *fan)*; the *rime* is the vowel sound and any following consonants of a syllable or word (e.g., *an* in *fan).*

orthoprint awareness The recognition of a spelling pattern in a word

out-of-context instruction Instruction that is done outside the context of meaningful reading or writing experiences

phoneme The smallest unit of sound in speech

phonemic awareness The ability to hear and distinguish individual sounds or phonemes in spoken words; the ability to blend, segment, and manipulate these phonemes

phonics A code-based component of reading instruction based on phoneme-grapheme associations

phonological awareness An understanding of the sounds and the structure of spoken language, including rhyming, blending, segmenting, deleting, and substituting words, syllables, and sounds

prefix One or more letters or sounds that are added to the beginning of a word and which change the meaning or grammatical function of the word (e.g., *re* in *rewrite, pre* in *preview)*

print awareness An understanding of the orthographic (print) nature of written language; the ability to recognize and identify syllables and words

rime See *onset/rime*

recoding The transformation of a printed grapheme or word into its speech form

root word The base word that remains after all prefixes and suffixes are removed (e.g., *friend* in *unfriendly).*

schema The prior knowledge and experiences that students bring to a learning situation and to which they relate and connect new information

semantic cues Cues taken from the general meaning of a story or text that readers use to help them figure out unknown words

structural analysis The identification of word elements, such as compound words, root words, prefixes, suffixes, and syllabication patterns

suffix One or more letters or syllables that are added to the end of a word and which change the meaning or grammatical function of the word (e.g., *less* in *sleepless*, *er* in *teacher*)

syllabication The strategy of dividing words into syllables, often used to assist with pronunciation

syntax cues Cues drawn from a reader's understanding of grammatical structures, word order, and language patterns within text that are used to help the reader figure out unknown words

synthetic phonics An instructional approach that introduces individual grapheme-phoneme correspondences before blending them to form syllables or whole words

whole language "A concept that embodies both a philosophy of language development and the instructional approaches embedded within, and supportive of, that philosophy…This concept includes the use of real literature and writing in the context of meaningful, functional, and cooperative experiences in order to develop in students motivation and interest in the process of learning" (Bergeron 1990)